𝔇aily 𝔗ele𝔤raph

Guide to the
COMMON MARKET

edited by Walter Farr

COLLINS LONDON & GLASGOW

William Collins Sons & Co. Ltd.
London & Glasgow

First published February, 1972
Reprinted April, 1972

© *Daily Telegraph*
ISBN 0 00 412011 6
Printed in Great Britain for the Publishers by
Richard Clay (The Chaucer Press), Ltd.,
Bungay, Suffolk

Contents

Contributors

Walter Farr, Common Market Correspondent, *Daily Telegraph*
Blake Baker, Industrial Correspondent
Clifford German, Deputy City Editor
Roland Gribben, Business Correspondent
W. D. Thomas, Agricultural Correspondent
Peter Duffy, 'Questor'
John Powell, City Office
    and *Daily Telegraph* correspondents throughout Europe

Editor's Preface

This is an impartial guide to the Common Market compiled to meet the needs of the many specialist and non-specialist readers who despite, or because of, the great debate still do not fully understand what it is that Britain is joining.

It combines for the first time in a single volume, a clearly worded and non-partisan description of the Common Market: showing how it works and how it began; an article-by-article layman's guide to the Treaty of Rome and the terms under which Britain accepts it and is prepared to adjust to its rules; a survey of each of the ten member states of an enlarged Market and expert analyses of the impact of entry in the factories, on the farms and on the people of Britain and Ireland.

For the many who still have serious doubts about the European venture, the chapters describing the checks and balances in the decision-making process in Brussels and assessment of how Britain's commitments work in practice will be of special interest. After watching all five British ministers responsible for Market negotiations in action – Heath, Brown, Chalfont, Thomson and Rippon – I am convinced that the final agreement achieved by the Tories is not very different from that which a Labour government would have accepted if President de Gaulle had not vetoed its application. Mr. Heath and Mr. Christopher Soames did well to reach the understanding with President Pompidou that Britain can veto any decision by the Council which is contrary to its vital interests.

As a result of that ultimate safeguard, Mr. Heath and Mr. Rippon were confident that they could persuade enough MPs to rise above suspicions and accept the consequential legislation which must be voted by Autumn, 1972, if Britain is to keep to the entry time-table.

Thanks are due to James Mallory, Collins reference department editor who was responsible for the production of the Guide. To keep readers fully informed of the many new developments in all sectors of the Market and of moves towards integration in other fields, new editions may be published as required. The list of contents of the Guide shows at a glance the magnitude of the step Britain is preparing to take on New Year's Day, 1973.

In the enlarged Community, the wrangling and crises over farm products will doubtless continue. However, they may be over-shadowed by decisions now being prepared in the Community institutions for using them to mould common European and defence policies so that it will become clear to the public that the European venture is much more than a business arrangement. Here, what Britain does may be decisive. If it decides to be represented in Brussels decision-making institutions and in the Strasbourg Parliament by leading politicians and diplomats, its partners will follow that lead. The best of the political and defence aims of the founders may then have been achieved.

The Community is a peaceful revolution, moving usually at the pace of its slowest, most hesitant members, which can, if Britain supplies the right kind of leadership, ultimately unite most of Europe. Ensuring that this revolution is beneficial there is a need not only for good government but for constructive opposition, first of course in Westminster but later in a strengthened European Parliament as well, in which men such as Enoch Powell and Sicco Mansholt exchange opposing ideas, or Harold Wilson and Roy Jenkins with Willy Brandt or Jean François Deniau.

As they face the challenge of the Market, Britain's ministers, parliamentarians, industrialists, business and professional men, and the public will find it helpful to have the basic facts contained in this Guide close at hand – not only related to their own special interests but on the Community as a whole. Britain's new commitments in the Market mean that the basic facts about the Ruhr, Flanders or the Mezzogiorno are now just as important to the lives of the British as the basic facts about Birmingham, Newcastle or Aberdeen. Europe is all of us.

Walter Farr

1

WHAT IS THE COMMON MARKET?

The Common Market is a community of independent states which have united their national markets in a single trading, farming and industrial system embracing a large part of Western Europe. It can, if all its members agree, be used as the basis for some form of future political union.

Six countries set up the Market by signing the Treaty of Rome on March 25, 1957, and putting it into force on January 1, 1958: *France, West Germany, Italy, The Netherlands, Belgium* and *Luxembourg*.

Four countries signed the Treaty of Accession on January 22, 1972, agreeing subject to votes by their Parliaments during 1972 to join the Common Market on January 1, 1973: *United Kingdom, Irish Republic, Denmark* and *Norway*.

Under the Rome Treaty rules, now being applied by the Six, manufactured and farm goods, workers, capital and many professional services, and to some extent tourists, move freely between the member states on the basis of common policies and laws made by common institutions in Brussels. Its common agricultural policy means that the cost of bread, butter or meat is fixed on the basis of a common price policy.

There is a common budget to which all member states contribute. This budget has been mainly used to help the farmers under the common farm policy but it may be applied to other sectors. A European Court enforces Market rules and it is agreed that, ultimately, there may be a directly-elected European Parliament. Coal, iron and steel have been put under common authorities; nuclear research promotion is under joint administration.

By 1970, member states had doubled their exports and now comprise the world's largest trading group.

It is called a common market because its member states are surrounded by a protective 'wall' of common customs duties within which there is free movement of goods. A firm in any one member state can therefore buy and sell in all other members almost as freely as it buys and sells across county boundaries in its own national market.

It is also called a community because, under the Treaty, its institutions were set up in the European Economic Community (EEC).

The Community method of decision-making which is used to run the Market has established a new political relationship between independent countries. Ministers of their national governments hold regular meetings in Brussels to exercise what are called 'community powers' for reaching decisions on Market policy. A minister can veto any proposal which affects his country's vital interests. However, once a decision is taken in Brussels it is automatically binding on all member states.

One of the most important results of this close, continuous relationship is that it provides a permanent basis (as far as is possible between fully independent countries). Firms can therefore make long-term plans with greater confidence than is possible under ordinary inter-governmental trade agreements. The founders hoped that as ministers developed the habit of thinking and acting together they would begin to use the Market's institutions, or similar ones, to agree on common action in other fields.

The Six first decided to implement plans for full economic and monetary union with a common currency by 1980.

They also began holding regular meetings of foreign ministers in an attempt to harmonise foreign policies. It was hoped that they would eventually agree on common foreign policies by using the same decision-making process which had led to common marketing policies. Many Market ministers and officials wanted a single foreign policy so that a large part of Europe would speak with one voice in influencing world affairs. The ultimate vision of the founders of the Market was that it would open the way for a Western European economic and political union which could also lead to an understanding with Eastern Europe.

However, the immediate and primary objective is to develop and consolidate a dynamic, expanding Market.

The Six created the Market's trading area, technically known as a customs union, by abolishing gradually trade barriers at their frontiers so that it became the sum of their national markets. These barriers mainly consisted of customs duties (tariffs) imposed on goods moving from one state to the other. At the same time a trade barrier (the common external tariff) was placed around the Market, thereby subjecting goods from the rest of the world to the same customs duty, regardless of the port of arrival. Market member states therefore trade with each other on a duty-free basis while protecting themselves from competitors outside it.

The Common Market gives a businessman whose firm is inside it three important advantages:

First, he has direct duty-free access to three or four times as many potential customers as he has in his own national market. Common rules for ensuring fair competition between firms and for co-ordinating tax, transport and other policies of member states generally mean that he can compete throughout the Market on an equal base regardless of nationality. As he can count on a big 'home' market of 250-million customers, his firm if it is making such things as cars or washing machines can have longer production runs. A greater quantity of goods can therefore be produced for the money the firm spends on research and various overheads. Its products can thus be made more cheaply and be more competitive in world markets.

Second, he has a substantial trading advantage over competitors sending goods into the Market from countries outside it. As they pay duties on their goods at the Market's outer 'wall', he can undersell them.

Third, his firm could benefit from the plans to make the Market the basis for close co-operation and perhaps integration of advanced technology, as in the need to pool investment and knowhow in making such things as aircraft, nuclear reactors, space vehicles, computers and weapons. It was proposed that this should be done by agreeing on a common industrial policy applied by the institutions in Brussels.

Abolition of the trade barriers between the member states means, of course, that a firm in any one of them, enjoying the three advantages listed above, is exposed to the full force of competition from industries throughout the Market. Whether this is an advantage or not depends on the firm's efficiency and enterprise. Under the entry terms it was agreed that almost all trade barriers between Britain and the Six would be abolished by 1975, assuming that Britain joined by January 1, 1973. By 1975, therefore, British firms, while gaining full access to the Common Market, will compete on an equal footing in Britain with firms in the rest of the Common Market.

The entry terms also mean that in some respects British firms will face increased competition in Britain from goods exported to this country by firms in countries outside the Market. This is because it was agreed under the entry terms to allow the Common Market's outer 'wall' (common external tariff) to be placed around Britain so that it replaces its national tariff against the rest of the world. The Market's 'wall' of duties on industrial goods is in many respects lower than Britain's national 'wall', thus enabling some exporters from the U.S., Japan and other countries to sell in Britain at lower prices.

Under the Treaty of Accession for entry into the Common

Market, signed in January, 1972, Britain agreed to be bound, with certain exceptions, by three treaties. These have set up three distinct but interlocked Communities to which the Six belong. They are:

> *The European Economic Community* (EEC), which has created and run the greater part of the Common Market since it came into force under the Rome Treaty in January, 1958.
>
> *The European Atomic Energy Community* (Euratom), set up at the same time as the EEC by a separate Rome Treaty. This promotes the use of atomic energy for peaceful purposes and has formed a common market for nuclear materials and equipment.
>
> *The European Coal and Steel Community* (ECSC), set up by the Treaty of Paris (signed in April, 1951); it began functioning in August, 1952. It placed the coal, steel, iron-ore and scrap resources of the Six in a common market and provided a working model for the wider common market created by the EEC.

All three Communities come under the same decision-making institutions in Brussels, and all are generally referred to as the Common Market or the European Community.

HOW THE COMMON MARKET WORKS

The Common Market's Economic, Coal and Steel and Atomic Energy Communities are run through two main institutions on which are nationals of all member states:

The Council of Ministers This is the Common Market's supreme decision-making body. Member states are usually represented at all its important meetings by their foreign ministers. When a decision involves a major policy act in a field other than foreign affairs the Council can include the minister responsible in that field, e.g. finance ministers for decisions concerned with economic and monetary union, ministers of agriculture for farm policy, etc. The foreign ministers take turns as President (chairman) of the Council for a six-month period. Meetings are usually held in Brussels, which has become the provisional capital of the Common Market, or in Luxembourg. By the 1970s it had become the practice to take all important decisions by unanimous vote (the Rome Treaty provided that there should be majority voting to speed up decision-making). Each member state therefore, in effect, can exercise a veto.

The Commission Its main task is to initiate and draw up proposals for Common Market policies and to table them in the Council at which it must be represented. The Commission is also an executive for implementing the decisions taken by the Council, such as those for running the common agricultural policy (CAP). Another of its tasks is to ensure, with the help of the European Court, that the Rome Treaty is not violated by states, institutions or individuals.

Under the terms for Britain's entry it was agreed that the Commission should be enlarged from nine members to fourteen (two being British). It decides by majority vote. Important decisions affecting the running of the Market must all be based on Commission proposals. Its members are appointed by unanimous agreement of Common Market governments. Before taking office they swear in the European Court that they will at no time be influenced in the policy moulding and implementing or decision-making process by national government or national interest; they are committed to act as 'Europeans'. The Commission has what is called 'its own power of decision' not only to initiate and, after a Council decision, implement policies but also to impose fines on firms considered to have broken the Common Market rules on fair competition. It has its own financial resources for running the common farm system, in the sense that money obtained by charging customs and other duties at the Market's outer tariff 'wall' is paid directly into a common Commission-controlled budget. The Council by unanimous vote only can take a measure amounting to an amendment of a Commission proposal. The Commission can be dismissed by the Common Market's Parliamentary Assembly, but not by the Council.

Neither the Council nor the Commission has power to use a police force or troops to implement a decision. Enforcement of a decision is the responsibility of the authorities within the member states. Therefore, although the institutions in Brussels have to some extent a federal appearance, they do not constitute a federal government. The powers they exercise are neither confederal nor federal. They are community powers and could only be transformed into federal power by unanimous agreement of the member governments and national legislatures.

The pooling of national sovereignty in the Brussels institutions creates what is regarded as a higher or shared sovereignty. Decisions flowing from this shared sovereignty are binding on member states only to the extent needed to create a market comparable in size and competitive power with, say, the United States. As the whole Market works ultimately on a voluntary basis, members are, in one sense, lending their sovereignty, since they can rescind if they have grounds for deciding that other members or any of the Market's institutions are breaking the rules. The belief by the early 1970s that the Community process was 'irreversible', has relegated this mechanism to the role of a safety valve, necessary but unlikely to be used.

The sovereignty involved at Brussels is greater than any yet pooled by independent countries but the Six felt that it was justified because there was no other way, short of total union, to ensure a stable, lasting Market. Apart from the carefully defined sections of sovereignty which have been merged under the Community Treaties each member maintains full powers and rights as an independent state. While firmly embracing its members, the system cannot crush them or undermine their national identities. The guiding principle is unity in diversity. This was reaffirmed by Mr. Edward Heath's and President Pompidou's declaration in 1971 that any proposal tabled in the Common Market Council affecting a member state's vital interests can be vetoed by that state's Council minister. This arrangement dates from 1965 when President de Gaulle ordered his ministers and top officials to boycott the Market's institutions, claiming that the Commission was trying to use them to impose federal powers on its members against their will. The boycott was ended by an agreement to disagree. At a meeting in Luxembourg, the French foreign minister made it clear in what has become known as the Luxembourg declaration that France reserved the right to veto any Council decision affecting its vital interests, i.e. to oppose a majority vote. Its five partners refused to abolish the majority voting rule but agreed that on issues affecting a country's vital interests the aim should be a unanimous vote. The Luxembourg meeting did not make a legally-binding decision: it is best described as a tacit understanding. As the Commission was not present at the meeting it was not, technically, a session of the Market Council. As the Heath–Pompidou pronouncement in 1971 was based on the Luxembourg declaration, it was therefore not in a strictly legal sense a full safeguard against the use of majority voting on a vital issue. It was, however, tolerated by others in the Market who would have preferred full majority voting, because they felt that for the time being it was in the long-term interests of the Community to accommodate Britain, thereby making it easier for it to join.

This willingness to dilute has been shown in other important ways, notably over the proposals for closer political unity. A direct confrontation which might endanger the whole Community venture or delay important progress in another field is often avoided. Thus, in the case of majority voting, France's partners avoided a direct confrontation with President de Gaulle while pressing on with other means of developing unity which suited him, such as the common farm policy. Leaders of some of the member states, and those members of the Commission who favour majority voting, believe that this will evolve gradually, as the Brussels institutions encourage them to work more and more closely together. It seemed clear, however, that any member state could, by using France's boycotting procedure, block any move in this direction.

It is open to member states at any time to decide, through the Council of Ministers, to change the Rome or Paris Treaties. These the Six agreed in principle to merge, having already merged their main institutions, and to draw up a new treaty. If this decision is implemented, Britain as a member would have as much say as any other member in maintaining or increasing the powers delegated to Brussels institutions.

The main decisions made by the Council of Ministers are called regulations and, as they are automatically binding on all member states no ratification of them is required by national legislatures. Part of the consequential legislation put before the Commons in 1972 would bring British practice into line so that the Community regulations would have direct internal effect in Britain.

It is generally recognised that the success of Community or Common Market decision-making has been the result of the system by which proposals and compromise plans are exchanged between Council and Commission. If the Council becomes deadlocked, the Commission, acting for the Community as a whole, breaks the deadlock by changing the proposal so that it meets some or all of the demands of the countries which caused the impasse; or it may introduce a new, more acceptable proposal which avoids meeting the original demands by adopting a new approach to the problem. The new proposal may even include a large part of the old one plus a plan which would give the opposing countries important benefits in another sector of the Market. The size of the Market does facilitate success in counter-balancing demands. It is this power of the Commission to continue the dialogue with new proposals that distinguishes the Community system from the inter-governmental method of decision-making in other international organisations, e.g. the Council of the North Atlantic Treaty Organisation (NATO), various organisations which aimed at European unity such as Western European Union (WEU) and the Council of Europe, and the United Nations.

Although all important Common Market decisions are taken by voluntary consent, ministers sitting in the Council feel what is often called the 'pull' of the Community. To withdraw or block decisions could mean losing a considerable benefit already acquired, or to come, through the Common Market.

The Commission, backed by a staff of 9-thousand, has great persuasive powers. Its greatest strength is its capacity to act impartially. A group of Commission members, or the head of it, is not likely to try to press through policies damaging to a member state, for their role is to act as Europeans furthering the interests of the Market as a whole and not acting as nationals of their own countries.

Similarly, a member of the Council of Ministers, though he may be under great pressure in his own country to try to push through something favouring an important sector of its economy, will try to avoid imposing partisan policies knowing that the Council could soon be considering Market policies which adversely affect interest groups in his country.

An important safeguard against the Commission opposing the interests of any member state is the Committee of Permanent Representatives, which, by established Brussels practice, will consist of the ambassadors to the Community of the ten members. The Committee vets proposals put to the Council and challenges any point likely to be unacceptable to a member state.

The European Court of Justice, which helps the Commission in fulfilling its role of watchdog to ensure full application of the Common Market rules, comprises judges from the member states, one of whom will be British. A further safeguard is the European Parliament in which it is agreed there must be 36 Parliamentarians from Westminster. This Parliament has been mainly a consultative body with very limited budgetary powers and has acted as a forum for expressing views on Community policies rather than for deciding their content. Its members however would not hesitate to bring maximum pressure on the Brussels institutions if they were felt to be acting against the best interests of citizens of the member states. The Treaties authorise the Parliament to dismiss the Commission. It was recognised by the early 1970s that this was a valuable safeguard in the sense that it meant that the Commission had to appear before the Parliament and give an account of its policies so that they could be explained and assessed.

Britain and Italy made a joint declaration in 1969 that they would try to strengthen the European Parliament by giving it the power to create, or influence the moulding of, policies and the means of implementation. In other words, in those sectors covered by the Common Market and by any policies flowing from its institutions, the European Parliament would legislate on a Continent-wide

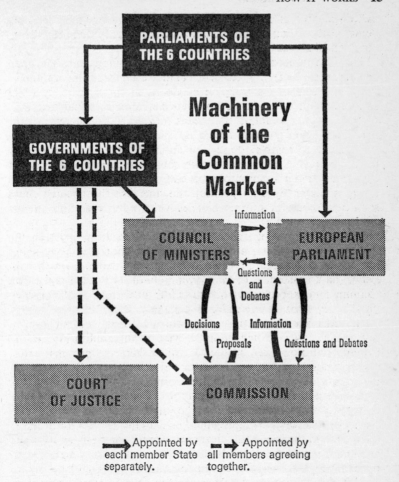

Machinery of the Common Market

PARLIAMENTS OF THE 6 COUNTRIES

GOVERNMENTS OF THE 6 COUNTRIES

COUNCIL OF MINISTERS

EUROPEAN PARLIAMENT

Information

Questions and Debates

COURT OF JUSTICE

COMMISSION

Decisions

Information

Proposals

Questions and Debates

Appointed by each member State separately.

Appointed by all members agreeing together.

basis much as the Westminster Parliament legislates for the nation. It was recognised, however, that great care should be taken to ensure that the European Parliament should not, apart from those issues concerned with running the Market, undermine the sovereign rights of the national legislatures. Constitutional authorities maintain that, despite the binding nature of the regulations made by the Council, the national legislature could request members of its government to send the minister back to Brussels to change them. Such a crisis currently appears unlikely in view of the right to veto any measure before it can become the law of the Community.

There are therefore checks and balances at every stage in the Community system and more are contemplated. There are also checks and balances in the minds of most of the men running it. During the first fourteen years the Market's leaders, men such as Sicco Mansholt of the Netherlands, head of the common farm system, his compatriot and one of the founders of the Common Market, Joseph Luns, and Jean François Deniau, member of the Commission responsible for British entry negotiations, repeatedly showed a sense of moderation.

As important as the qualities of the men running the Brussels institutions is the European spirit in which decisions are taken. This has to be felt in and around the Market's Council chamber to be fully understood. Foreign ministers and those for finance and agriculture of all member states frequently participate, together with the leaders and experts of the Commission, in Market Council sessions as if they are members of a European cabinet. Many know their opposite numbers in other national governments better than they know colleagues in their own national cabinets. Council sessions took up 80 days of every year from the late 1960s onwards.

No-one had expected that when the full rules of the Market came into effect in 1970 (at the end of the 12-year period of adjustment) that the Brussels compromise machine would become a European government. Indeed some national governments continued to act unilaterally, little regarding their partners' best interests. This led for instance to a partial, and it was hoped, temporary, restoration of barriers to the free flow of agricultural goods at the frontiers between them. Such setbacks did not surprise the founders of the Market. They had always recognised that the merging of the agricultural systems of independent states would be extremely difficult, particularly in view of the fact that it meant in the early stages that individual farm crises would be merged into one big Market crisis. All felt, however, that the Market Council had enough powers to stimulate not only the Six but the whole of Western Europe towards greater prosperity.

The institutions in Brussels have three different but interrelated objectives. Firstly, they run the Common Market; secondly, they are completing those parts of it called for by the Treaties which, because one or more members raised difficulties, have yet to be implemented; thirdly, they are trying to bind members together in new ways which, though not legally required under the Treaties, could help the business side of the Community and lead, perhaps, to closer political unity. In addition, during the 1960s and early 1970s, they had to keep breaking off from decision-making in these three fields to negotiate on the enlarging of the Market to include Britain on all aspects of foreign trade policy and to establish or consolidate links with the greater part of Black Africa, the Mediterranean, and Commonwealth countries in the Caribbean, the Pacific and Indian Oceans, and the Far East.

All this explains why in the Brussels Council and Commission meetings there were so many crises and day-and-night sessions ('marathons'). It often happened, for instance, that a one day or night Brussels agenda might include the level of the common farm prices for all farm products for the coming harvest, a new move to implement Treaty provisions for creating rules for European firms, the next step in completing a common trade policy for the Six in their dealings with the Soviet Union, and the time-table for adjusting the rules of the common budget to Britain and the other applicant countries until the 1980s. It became general practice, when the Council or the Commission was deadlocked, to agree to set a 'deadline' for final agreement on a compromise still to be worked out. When the deadline was not met members spent hours accusing each other of breaking it while ignoring the substance of the problem. This led anti-Marketeers in the Six and elsewhere and some who had been strong supporters of the Market to conclude that the whole system was too complicated and that it was generating more disunity than unity. At times it was. Yet experience in the 20 years since the Community system was first applied, with the setting up of the Coal and Steel Community, has shown that almost all meetings, even some of the worst of the crises, have resulted in an edging forward to a solution of the problems of one or all of the members. In this sense a Brussels crisis has never been considered as serious as an inter-governmental diplomatic crisis. This is because the Treaties provide for regular sessions.

In any case, even if tempted to stay away, a minister knows that there must be another meeting of some kind to deal with the day-to-day, but often extremely important, decisions in running the Market. Cancellation of the meetings would cause the Market to lose momentum and all would stand to lose money. This was clearly shown when President de Gaulle boycotted the institutions. Even he had to agree, though the chair of the French minister remained empty at the Council meeting, that decisions on running the Market should continue to be made by an exchange of letters between Brussels and Paris. When the ministers meet again, as was the case after de Gaulle's boycott, the old deadlocked issues are still on the agenda. By then, however, the experts have worked on them. Some are left by general agreement on one side to be tackled months, even years later. Or, entirely new ones are put onto the agenda so that positive decision-making can be resumed. Finally, a collection of proposals is usually formulated, including decisions conceding certain points to the country which caused the deadlock.

Ministers meeting in an ordinary international conference would not be briefed with compromises of a kind produced by Commission experts capable of taking a detached, overall view of the problems. Their aim is to look at them as far as possible with the long-term interests of the Community and therefore of all its members in mind. A country taking part in an ordinary international conference or organisation is more likely to decide to break off the talks and act unilaterally not because this suits its long-term interests but to gain a short-term political advantage at home by forcing a stalemate on a decision which, even if sensible, is opposed by a large part of its electorate.

The classic example of how the policy-making system developed by the Council and Commission strikes a fair balance of advantages for all was the sudden surge of decisions in the great 1969 marathon session which produced the unprecedented package of agreements for completing the Market, extending its system to other fields and opening negotiations with Britain. West Germany agreed to the setting up of the common budget, which meant that its taxpayers were committed to helping to subsidise French and Dutch agriculture. The French gave way to German demands to begin negotiating with Britain, Ireland, Denmark and Norway (thus opening the way for big gains for West Germany's industries). The Dutch gave way by diluting their proposals for granting sweeping powers to the European Parliamentary Assembly. Italy, by threatening to hold up all these proposals, won big concessions from the others on wine and tobacco. After maximum pressure from their partners, Belgium and Italy delayed applying their value-added taxes. Luxembourg held on to its rights as a Market administrative centre against the combined pressure of most other members and a large part of the Commission. Much of the astonishing package deal which opened the way for British entry was possible because member states, with the help of the Commission, saw that it was well worthwhile to give way in one particular sector and short-term political benefits were waived.

Sometimes a proposal which appears to be perfectly reasonable and meets requirements laid down in the Treaty is held up for months, even years, on some relatively minor technicality. Then suddenly the word goes around the Brussels lobbies that two or three of the members have had a private talk and that an all-night session is planned. Usually things are brought to a head because one country feels that it has been completely isolated by all the others and the Commission. On almost all occasions when this has happened the isolated one has been shown to be taking a stand directly against the general interest of the Community and, very often, in the long term against its own interest. Care is often taken to avoid putting too much pressure on a government facing elections. When the Council finally is agreed, it is often after lengthy nocturnal telephone calls between ministers and their heads of government. Often they agree to accept the compromise, subject to a final decision by their national government.

In judging the Market's confused, often baffling, meetings it is important to keep in mind the fact that members are only just beginning to come to grips with the most difficult problems involved in this, the first attempt ever made to unite independent European countries by voluntary assent. It would of course be much neater if one or other of the larger powers were to impose solutions. Some countries have tried to do this (notably France, in the Gaullist era) and very nearly succeeded. Community institutions are more enduring than Community men and they will have the last word. A national leader can, the founders admit, succeed in bullying his partners for a time; but they maintain that in the long run the Community system, the 'continuing process', succeeds because it demonstrates to the public in his country that nationalistic policies are not in its best interest. Many a minister at Brussels Council meetings has felt like storming out and giving up the whole venture. When de Gaulle's Foreign Minister, Maurice Couve de Murville, did in fact do this by his boycott of the institutions in the 1960s a large section of French public opinion turned against the Gaullists. It is now generally accepted that any government which tries to break out of the Market would face a domestic political crisis. It has, the founders claim, become 'part of the political scenery' and a large section of the public instinctively feels that it is the best system yet devised to prevent a return to nationalistic rivalries. Sir Alec Douglas-Home has said that if the Common Market institutions had existed in the early part of the century both world wars would have been avoided. For what they regard as good political as well as good economic reasons, Market ministers feel 'condemned to agree'. Many newcomers to Brussels wonder why there has to be so much confusion and unintelligible wrangling before the ministers agree. Why do some of them appear to be behaving like members of a European federal government and others like violent nationalists? Having made a set of rules and found that it is difficult to apply them, why try to make new, more complicated rules? Why try to extend the Brussels rules to new fields when they have not yet been fully applied to the fields defined in the Treaties? Is the haggling over basic principles really necessary? Why not simplify the decision-making system or even go back to the old inter-governmental methods so that everyone knows exactly where he stands and the public can begin to grasp what it is all about? Is it ever likely, the newcomer wonders, that machinery which cannot fix reasonable prices for food, can ever be used to help to decide issues related to peace and war?

The answers to these questions lie in the origins of the Common Market and of the three Communities on which it is based.

THE ORIGINS OF THE COMMON MARKET

The Common Market was formed on the basis of a compromise between European federalists and a miscellaneous group which came to be known as the European functionalists. Each wanted to unite Europe but they differed on how and when it should be done.

This explains why the Market institutions sometimes appear to tend towards full political union while at other times some of the member states appear determined to transform them into international secretariats such as those in the North Atlantic Treaty Organisation (NATO), the Western European Union or many sections of the United Nations.

The federalists decided at secret meetings organised by the Resistance movements during the Second World War and at great rallies soon after the fighting ended that the nations of Europe should be merged to form a 'super-state'. It would include a federal government with a federal reserve bank and federal armed forces. A European parliament would be formed on the basis of direct elections in which MPs would be chosen to represent each nation state in much the same way that the members of the United States Congress are chosen to represent each state.

The idea of European unity was not new. Historic precedents range from the Holy Roman Empire of Charlemagne to the territorial conquests of Napoleon and Hitler. It assumed a new importance with the devastation and suffering in Europe left at the end of the War. The greater part of the Continent had become a kind of no-man's-land across which the U.S. and the Soviet Union were initiating another struggle, the Cold War. Survivors of Hitler's war, victors and vanquished alike, felt a deep sense of shame and bewilderment when they realised the full horror of the crimes committed:

there were 15-million dead, an unknown number of them tortured or gassed in German concentration camps, 60-million refugees, millions near starvation level, two-million wrecked homes.

The federalists believed that the root cause lay in the system of self-interested nation states. They saw Europe as a collection of twenty or thirty fragmented nations, most of them separated by huge trade barriers, each acting unilaterally to change the balance of power until there was nothing but a power vacuum left. It was this, the federalists believed, that had led to the economic collapse between the two world wars and created mass unemployment which, in Germany, Hitler was able to exploit. Only a total merger, the federalists argued, could prevent the rise of another dictator and a third world war. The symbols of nationalism were thought to be bankrupt and in danger of being captured by communists or neo-nazis.

The functionalists' ideas were less drastic. They favoured a step-by-step advance towards unity. Nation states would retain their independence but would pool enough sovereignty to allow institutions to exercise 'limited functions but real powers' over one sector of their economies or over certain industries. After each step, most of them advocated a long pause to assess the practical functioning of the institutions before deciding on common action in another sector. There were functionalists who wanted only to form organisations for international co-operation such as joint secretariats firmly under the control of governments; others wanted bodies which would fully integrate their economies as a step towards a loose form of federation in the distant future. The latter argued that inter-govern-mental co-operation was not viable because any one government involved could break it up in much the same way that the old alliances between the wars had broken up. (They expect this to happen eventually in NATO, following France's major break with it.)

Among the federalists and functionalists were Europe's ablest politicians and economists. Many belonged to christian democrat parties and all wanted Europe to assume a new world role. All looked to Britain for leadership. Winston Churchill was the first of its political leaders to urge them to unite. What was needed, he said in his speech in Zurich in 1946, was 'a kind of United States of Europe'. Later he went so far as to propose that this united Europe should be backed by a European army in the hands of a federal ministry of defence. 'This noble continent,' Churchill said, 'is the origin of most of the culture, arts, philosophy and science of both ancient and modern times. If Europe were once united in the sharing of its common inheritance there would be no

limit to the happiness, to the prosperity and glory which its three-
to four-hundred million people would enjoy.' The War and its
horror camps was, he said 'a horrible retrogression' back to the
Middle Ages without their chivalry and without their faith.

> 'All this could be ended at a single stroke . . . The peoples of
> Europe have only got to wake up one morning and resolve to be
> happy and free by becoming one family of nations, banded together
> from the Atlantic to the Black Sea for mutual aid and protection.
> One spasm of resolve! One single gesture! . . . I am now going to
> say something that will astonish you. The first step in the re-
> creation of the European family must be a partnership between
> France and Germany.'

At a London rally of the United European Movement, which he
helped to create, the then Leader of the Opposition said: 'We hope
to reach again a Europe purged of the slavery of ancient days, in
which men will be proud to say: "I am a European".'

The federalists looked to him as their leader. No politician has
ever proclaimed the federal vision with such force and clarity. His
words left the great mass of the people on the Continent in no doubt
that this was the right road.

When the Continental federalists called for a European federal
parliament, France supported the idea. Britain rejected it: the
Labour government agreed only to the creation of the Council of
Europe, which had a federal appearance. MPs from Britain, France
and many other Western European countries met in its European
Parliamentary Assembly and it was agreed that there should be a
European court to safeguard human rights. There were hopes that
the Council would gradually acquire some federal powers. In fact,
it was so closely controlled by national governments through its
Committee of Ministers, including Ernest Bevin, that it became
little more than a sounding board for ideas for uniting Europe in
other ways.

To the dismay of the federalists, when Churchill returned to
office, he made it clear that the great vision of a federal Europe
which he had proclaimed in Opposition was a union of nations on
the Continent. France and West Germany must, he said, shake
hands and the British would simply cheer from the sidelines. By then
Britain and a large part of Europe had begun an economic recovery
with the help of the American Marshall Aid plan. It had led to the
creation of an inter-governmental secretariat called the Organisation
for European Economic Co-operation (OEEC). This was much more
to Britain's taste. The new Conservative administration felt that
Britain was still a great world power and that federal or similar links

with the defeated nations across the Channel would not be in its best interests. Having stood alone during the War, it felt confident that Britain could continue to stand alone with the help of Commonwealth partners and a special relationship with the United States. It agreed to strengthen defence ties with the Continent through the Brussels Treaty and eventually to form the Western European Union with yet another Parliamentary Assembly similar to that of the Council of Europe and with institutions for overseeing German armaments; but again this would involve a conventional governmental secretariat.

The debate between the federalists and the functionalists on the Continent was brought to a head when the Soviet Union acquired a nuclear capability and the U.S. demanded that West Germany should be rearmed and brought into the Western alliance. The federalists, notably Jean Monnet, then head of France's national planning board, seized on one of the greatest of the Churchill ideas, his proposal for a reconciliation between France and Germany. Federal leaders had learnt from their failure to win real powers for the Council of Europe that the most effective tactic was the one proposed by the functionalists, to move forward to political unity step by step. The first step should then be Franco-German reconciliation but it had to go further than Churchill had suggested: it had to be given a cast-iron basis.

Monnet worked out a plan under which the whole of French and German iron, steel and coal resources, much of it concentrated at their common frontier, should be put under a common authority. This he saw as the beginning of a European federation, but to win the support of some of the functionalists, the system was called a community. Monnet proposed the creation of the European Coal and Steel Community to Robert Schuman, then France's Foreign Minister. No-one was better able to understand the need for a Franco-German reconciliation than Schuman. His family had lived in Alsace-Lorraine before the First World War. Because it had changed hands in two wars, Schuman had lived part of his life as if he were a German and therefore knew the agony and absurdity of the Franco-German quarrel. Schuman immediately accepted the Monnet plan. The French cabinet then adopted it. 'This Community,' Schuman said, 'is an instrument of peace which has about it a higher wisdom born of suffering.' He also recognised that it made sense economically. Only by pooling their mineral and other resources in a common market could the countries of Europe hope to compete against the American giant and be able to afford to make or buy the weapons needed in the nuclear age. Finally, and perhaps decisively, the binding together of the war-making industries of Germany and its neighbours would make it almost impossible for the Germans to start another war.

In his historic declaration (May, 1950) announcing the coal and steel plan, Schuman said:

> 'Europe will not be built all at once, or through a single compre-hensive plan. It will be built through concrete achievements, which will first create a *de facto* solidarity. The comity of European nations requires that the rivalry of France and Germany should be eliminated. Action should therefore first be concentrated on France and Germany. The French government proposes immediate action on a limited but decisive point: my government proposes to place the whole of the production of coal and steel in France and Germany under a common high authority in an organisation open to the participation of the other countries of Europe. The pooling of the production of coal and steel will immediately establish a common basis for economic development.
>
> 'It will change the destiny of these regions which for so long have been used for making the weapons of war of which they have been most frequently the victims. The solidarity between the two countries established by joint production will show that a war between France and Germany becomes not only unthinkable but materially impossible.
>
> 'Thus will be realised, simply and rapidly, the fusion of interests which are indispensable for establishing an economic community between countries long opposed by bloody conflict. This will establish the basis for a European federation indispensable for the safeguarding of peace.'

The Schuman declaration also made the point that Europe with greater economic power would be able to contribute more towards the development of Africa.

The preamble of the Treaty of Paris, signed a year later by France, West Germany, Italy, Holland, Belgium and Luxembourg, declared that they were:

> 'Resolved to substitute for historic rivalries a fusion of their essential interests, to establish by creating an economic community, the foundations of a broader and deeper community among peoples long divided by bloody conflicts; and to lay the bases of institutions capable of guiding their common destiny.'

In the Treaty itself, it was laid down that the members of the High Authority for running the coal and steel production of the member states 'shall refrain from any action incompatible with the supra-national character of their functions. . . . Each member state under-takes to respect this supra-national character and not to seek to influence the members of the High Authority in the performance of their task.'

Here then was the beginning of the Community system which now, in much more moderate form, is being used to run the full Common Market in the European Economic Community. Its aim, as Schuman said, was a federation but its method of advance was functional: not uniting Europe in one go, but by a series of moves. This immediately appealed to West Germany's Konrad Adenauer, Italy's Alcide de Gasperi, the Netherlands' Dr. Luns and other leaders of the Six. They saw it as a move, not only to prevent another European war, but to strengthen Europe in case a war was started by the Soviet Union.

While the 'supra-national' aspect was emphasised in the Treaty, it did not say that the intention of the members was to create a federation. This omission, it was explained, was intended as part of a compromise agreed upon with the functionalists.

Monnet became the first president of the Coal and Steel Community's High Authority. Like the Council of Europe and the WEU, the Community had its own Parliamentary Assembly and, like the Council, its own Court of Justice.

Encouraged by the success of the coal and steel market, the federalists then launched a plan for a European defence community with a European army on lines similar to the one Churchill had suggested but with a wholly federal government based on a European political community. The initiative had come mainly from France because it feared that West Germany, which was then being allowed to rearm, might once again turn on its neighbours. The French legislature, torn between a desire to tie the Germans into the Coal and Steel Community and a fear that France might again come under German domination, refused in 1954 to ratify the European defence community plan. This was the federalists' biggest failure. Britain, they felt, was partly to blame for refusing to join either the Coal and Steel Community or the European army.

Monnet immediately announced that he would resign from the Coal and Steel Community and formed the Action Committee for the United States of Europe. In close co-operation with Monnet, Johan Beyen of the Netherlands, Paul-Henri Spaak of Belgium and Luxembourg's Joseph Bech then produced plans for two more communities: the full Common Market as it now exists and the one for atomic energy (Euratom). After beginning with the economic field (coal and steel) and their unsuccessful attempt to move on to defence and political fields, the federalists had now, with the launching of the EEC and Euratom, gone back to economics.

The Rome Treaty which created EEC and Euratom was much more moderately worded than the Coal and Steel treaty. The word 'supra-national' was not used. The main decision-making body was not a high authority (comprising Eurocrats); the EEC and Euratom were to be run by the Council of Ministers on the basis of proposals from the Eurocrats. As ministers represented their national governments, this meant that in the Common Market and Euratom communities the emphasis was much less on the use of federal or federal-type power. Yet many of the founders of the Market insisted that the ultimate aim was still to move towards some form of federal government. The Rome Treaty preamble defined the aim as 'an ever closer union of the peoples of Europe'.

The diluting of the supra-national aspect was felt to be necessary partly because nationalism was rising as the Marshall Aid brought about recovery and memories of the War faded. It was also hoped that the emphasis on decisions between governments might attract British functionalists. Euratom was also looked upon as an attractive proposition for Britain in view of its great advances in the peaceful use of atomic energy. (At one time Euratom was expected to be more important than the EEC.) The British however once again refused to join the Six and even withdrew their observers from the Messina negotiations leading to the draft of the Common Market treaty. Many British officials in Continental capitals forecast that it would be a 'flop'.

In 1955 Britain tried to persuade West Germany to break away from the Common Market plan. Angered by what he regarded as deliberate sabotage, M. Spaak, who was in charge of the Market negotiations, reminded Anthony Eden that the main purposes of the Market were to solve the problem of a resurgent Germany. As a member of the Market, M. Spaak said, Germany would find it easier to control its nationalist extremists. It would also be less likely to approach the Soviet Union unilaterally in an effort to solve its problems without regard for the needs of the West as a whole.

After the Common Market was established (1957) Britain tried bringing it into a larger Western European free trade area. De Gaulle was quick to see that this plan, presented by Reginald Maudling, contained no common rules for helping French agriculture. For this and other reasons de Gaulle vetoed it. Britain then initiated the forming of the European Free Trade Association (EFTA), which eventually comprised Denmark, Sweden, Norway, Switzerland, Austria, Portugal, Finland and Iceland. Like those of the Common Market, the EFTA rules require the removal of customs duties between the members. The important difference is that EFTA countries continue to apply their own national customs duties towards the rest of the world. EFTA therefore, unlike the Market, is not surrounded by a unified outer 'wall' and is not able to encourage its members towards closer economic and political unity. One of its aims was to help the 'Outer Nine' countries of Europe to present a united front in the hope that one day they could come to terms with the Market.

The creation of EFTA meant that Western Europe was now economically, and to some extent politically, divided into two.

Monnet, after one of his many appeals to Britain to join the Six, rightly said: 'You British always find it difficult to accept principles and prefer to make your decisions on the basis of facts. We on the Continent first set out the principles believing that the facts will emerge later. They will emerge in our Communities and, when they do, you British will join us.' The facts did emerge. In its first few years the Market showed, by quadrupling trade between its members and stepping up their growth, that it was very different from any unity organisation yet.

This was not the only factor which led to second thoughts in London. President de Gaulle began trying to persuade his Market partners to move from economic unity to some form of political union. He had never made any secret of the fact that he saw the Market as helpful in the sense that it gave a boost to French agriculture and also as a possible instrument for the greater grandeur of France. It could enhance his policy of coolness towards the United States and co-operation with the Soviet Union. Drawings in the French press depicting him as emperor of Western Europe were not entirely fanciful. In 1960 he proposed holding meetings of Market heads of government. He said that, between the meetings of this 'High Political Council', a secretariat (with headquarters in Paris) would prepare plans for joint political decisions. Later de Gaulle went so far as to suggest 'organised co-operation between the Six while waiting to achieve, perhaps, an imposing confederation'. After long arguments in the Fouchet Committee, Dr. Luns made it clear that the Netherlands would never accept this or any other form of close political union unless Britain were a member. But the Six's heads of government decided in Bonn in 1961 'to give shape to the will for political union'.

What had shaken the anti-Marketeers in London was that the Six were excluding Britain from their political discussions. It was at this point that many in Whitehall realised that Britain could no longer afford simply to cheer or jeer from the sidelines. Was there not a danger that the Six, despite the stand taken by the Dutch, might make political decisions jointly which could further Soviet aims? Might not the Germans eventually run the Community of the Six? The Bonn declaration was not implemented, but de Gaulle was to make further attempts to dominate the Community politically.

In July, 1961, the Prime Minister, Mr. Macmillan, announced that Britain would begin negotiations with the Common Market to see if suitable terms could be achieved. The view in Whitehall was that it was better to put the emphasis on joining the Market than on the importance of being involved with the Six politically. This partly explains why most people still talk of the European venture as a business deal.

De Gaulle vetoed Britain's first application for entry even though, by 1963, the negotiations had clearly shown that reasonable terms could have been agreed upon. He suspected that Britain intended to sabotage the common agricultural policy which had not yet been completed in ways which were to give substantial help to French farmers. He also saw Britain as a 'Trojan horse' trying to break into the Market to transform it into an Anglo-American province. Finally, he feared that Britain and West Germany might combine against France. He often pointed out that France was in great danger of losing its national identity because some of its frontier areas were strongly influenced by its neighbours. There is also little doubt that de Gaulle still found it difficult to forgive Britain for rejecting many of his plans when he led the Free French in London during the Second World War.

Edward Heath, Britain's chief negotiator, had impressed the Six during the negotiations (1961–3) by his stubbornness and by his grasp of the Community's basic aims. He impressed them even more when the talks collapsed by immediately declaring that Britain, despite the veto, would not turn its back on Europe.

When Mr. Wilson applied for membership in 1967 de Gaulle used his veto again for the same reasons. The Labour government made it clear that its application remained on the Brussels conference table. De Gaulle's successor, Georges Pompidou, in what was regarded as one of the great acts of statesmanship, decided in 1971 to open the way for British entry on what appeared to be reasonable terms. Two of Britain's EFTA partners, Denmark and Norway, plus Ireland, it was agreed should join with it. The other six EFTA countries began negotiating for close links with the enlarged Market. Britain and the other three applicants also agreed to begin having regular foreign ministerial meetings immediately with the Six to discuss the harmonising of foreign policy. The Six had begun to hold meetings for this purpose in the framework of the Davignon Committee. It was set up after West German Chancellor Willy Brandt, one of the strongest 'Europeans', had said at a meeting of heads of government at The Hague in 1969: 'Our Community must not be a new power bloc, but an exemplary system which can serve as an element in the forging of a well-balanced pan-European peace settlement. . . . It must be understood afresh that Europe is more than a collection of market organisations and the young must realise that Europe is something other than the memory of a past of sombre glory.'

The Hague Conference communiqué contained some phrases which recalled the fervour of Monnet, Schuman and de Gasperi as they launched the first Community. It said:

> 'The heads of state [President Pompidou] and of governments . . . wish to reaffirm their belief in the political objectives which give the Community its meaning and purport, their determination to carry their undertaking through to the end, and their confidence in the final success of their efforts. . . . Entry upon the final stage of the Common Market means confirming the irreversible nature of the work accomplished by the three Communities. It also means paving the way for a united Europe capable of assuming its responsibilities in the world of tomorrow and of making a contribution commensurate with its traditions and its mission.'

As Dr. Luns, who did more than anyone else to make the successful Hague summit possible, said when it ended: 'It is now up to Britain . . .' In their discussions at The Hague the Six had in fact made it clear that they were deliberately slowing down the Community's political and, to some extent, its economic and monetary development until Britain joined.

The Six stressed that the future, not only of the Market but of the Community method, would largely depend on how Britain carried out, both in letter and spirit, the commitments it had accepted in the Treaties. What precisely these commitments are and the extent to which they affect the British domestic market and the economy generally are explained in the next chapters.

2

THE COMMON MARKET TREATIES

Britain's commitments as a member of the Common Market are established in eight groups of documents:

1. The Treaty signed in Rome in 1957 which formed the full Common Market (i.e. European Economic Community, EEC), together with a number of annexes, protocols and conventions spelling out special arrangements for certain products. This is usually referred to as the *Rome Treaty*.
2. The Treaty setting up the European Atomic Energy Community which, although it was also signed in Rome in 1957, is known generally as the *Euratom Treaty*.
3. The Treaty setting up the European Coal and Steel Community (ECSC) was signed in Paris in 1951 and is therefore called the *Paris Treaty*. It has a number of protocols and conventions attached to it dealing with such fields as the co-ordinating of energy policies of the member states.
4. The two treaties which amend the EEC, Euratom and ECSC Treaties are known as the Merger Treaty (which established a single Council and a single Commission) and the Budget Treaty. These came into force in 1967 and 1970 respectively.
5. The texts of some 15-hundred *regulations*, *directives* and general *decisions* made by the Common Market Council and Commission which, in accordance with the Treaties, automatically become binding on the member states. *Community laws*, as the regulations and directives are called, operate only in the fields covered by the Treaties, that is: customs duties; agriculture; free movement of labour, services and capital; transport; monopolies and restrictive practices; state aid for industry; and policy-making for the coal and steel and nuclear energy industries. By far the greater part of Britain's domestic or national laws therefore remains unchanged.
6. The *Treaty of Accession* to the Common Market, signed in January, 1972. This provides that Britain accedes to the three Communities. It then sets out in legal form certain modifications, or derogations, which, under the terms for British entry, will be made in the Treaties or in the regulations, directives and

decisions referred to above. These modifications have been made to meet Britain's special needs either during the period when it is adjusting to the Market rules or on a permanent basis.

7. Legislation presented to the British Parliament in 1972 generally known as *consequential legislation* to bring British law into line with the requirements of the Treaties and the regulations, directives and decisions flowing from them. Legislation is also needed to spell out Britain's acceptance that the Market Council has power, in fields covered by the Treaties, to make decisions which automatically come into force in this country.

8. The texts of the case law of the European Court of Justice.

Also drafts of Community policies flowing from the three Treaties or concerned with co-operation between member states in fields other than those covered by the Treaties. These include documents on the first steps towards a Community *regional policy*, a full *economic and monetary union, fuel and power and industrial policies, science and technology co-operation*, and the Davignon Committee (*common foreign policy*). The Six said British entry would mean 'accepting the Treaties and their political finality, decisions since they came into force and options taken on the Communities' development'.

The Commission is generally responsible for enforcing the Community law which has direct effect in Britain and the other member states. It has power in some cases to decide whether there has been an infringement and, in accordance with a quasi-judicial procedure, to impose penalties. These penalties, except in certain cases which could arise under the Euratom Treaty, are always monetary. Such a decision is subject to challenge before the European Court of Justice on which, it is agreed, there should be a British judge.

Thus, an individual or firm in Britain or any of the other members, wishing to know how the Market rules (and the way they have been interpreted) work in practice for a particular product or field of policy, would first consult the relevant Articles of the Treaty or Treaties and would then consult any section of the Accession Treaty which may have modified it to meet Britain's special needs. Then, they would read regulations, directives and decisions made on the basis of the relevant parts of the Treaties and finally would study any relevant decisions made by the European Court.

A firm wishing to assess the long-term prospects for a particular product in the Market, or for such things as company mergers or freeing of capital movements, is advised to consult the latest texts of new policies flowing from the Treaties or changes in old ones.

British experts who have gone through the documents listed above have emphasised that none of them raises any great difficulty. The many derogations from the strict application of various obligations to individual member states show that the principles of the Treaties are applied pragmatically and that due allowance is made for the particular circumstances of member states.

Authentic English texts of the Rome, Euratom and Paris Treaties and of the Treaty of Accession and related instruments are being made available in Britain for early 1972 at H.M.'s Stationery Office. Unofficial English translations of the Rome, Euratom and Paris Treaties and of regulations, directives, decisions and policies flowing from them may be obtained at several of H.M.'s Stationery Office bookshops.

The Treaty of Accession Preamble says Britain and the other nine states wish to pursue the Rome Treaty objectives and are '. . . determined in the spirit of the Community Treaties to construct an ever closer union among the peoples of Europe on the foundations already laid . . .' (See page 59.)

LAYMAN'S GUIDE TO THE TREATY OF ROME

The Rome Treaty which set up the full Common Market is the most important of the Community documents in the sense that its provisions and measures flowing from it have had the greatest immediate impact on member states. It is important, not only because it contains the basis of the Market, but because it outlines in general terms further policies which were intended to lead on to full economic union of the member states. It has often been called 'an outline Treaty'.

Whereas the other two Treaties lay down in detail precisely what rules are to be applied, the Common Market Treaty, apart from its provisions for removing trade barriers, leaves it to the Community institutions (primarily Council and Commission) to work out the precise arrangements in the main areas of economic activity.

Thus it leaves open the field of full economic union to be filled in without the necessity for new treaties or further ratification by national legislatures. A blank was left in the field of agricultural policy and, since the Treaty came into effect, it has been filled in by the corpus of secondary legislation on agriculture, comparable in its impact on the members to the corpus of rules contained in the Coal and Steel Treaty.

What follows is a layman's guide to the Rome Treaty giving the text or a full summary of the most important of its 248 Articles, and how they have been applied, together with notes in italics showing how under the entry terms they have been adapted or modified to meet Britain's requirements.

Treaty setting up the European Community, Rome, 25th March, 1957

PREAMBLE

HIS MAJESTY THE KING OF THE BELGIANS, THE PRESIDENT OF THE FEDERAL REPUBLIC OF GERMANY, THE PRESIDENT OF THE FRENCH REPUBLIC, THE PRESIDENT OF THE ITALIAN REPUBLIC, HER ROYAL HIGHNESS THE GRAND DUCHESS OF LUXEMBOURG, HER MAJESTY THE QUEEN OF THE NETHERLANDS,

DETERMINED to establish the foundations of an ever closer union among the European peoples,

RESOLVED to ensure by common action the economic and social progress of their countries by eliminating the barriers which divide Europe,

AFFIRMING as the essential objective of their efforts the constant improvement of the living and working conditions of their peoples,

RECOGNISING that the removal of existing obstacles calls for concerted action in order to guarantee steady expansion, balanced trade and fair competition,

ANXIOUS to strengthen the unity of their economies and to ensure their harmonious development by reducing the differences existing between the various regions and the backwardness of the less favoured regions,

DESIRING to contribute, by means of a common commercial policy, to the progressive abolition of restrictions on international trade,

INTENDING to confirm the solidarity which binds Europe and overseas countries and desiring to ensure the development of their prosperity, in accordance with the principles of the Charter of the United Nations,

RESOLVED to strengthen the cause of peace and liberty by thus pooling their resources and calling upon the other peoples of Europe who share their ideal to join in their efforts,

HAVE DECIDED to create a European Economic Community.

PART ONE—Principles

ARTICLE 1

By this Treaty, the High Contracting Parties set up among themselves a EUROPEAN ECONOMIC COMMUNITY.

ARTICLE 2

The Community shall have as its task, by setting up a common market and progressively approximating the economic policies of Member States, to promote throughout the Community an harmonious development of economic activities, a continuous and balanced expansion, an increase in stability, an accelerated raising of the standard of living and closer relations between the Member States belonging to it.

ARTICLE 3

For the purposes set out in Article 2, the activities of the Community shall include, on the conditions and in accordance with the time-table provided in this Treaty:

(a) the elimination, as between Member States, of customs duties and of quantitative restrictions in regard to the import and export of goods, as well as of all other measures having equivalent effect;

(b) the establishment of a common customs tariff and of a common commercial policy towards third countries;

(c) the abolition, as between Member States, of obstacles to freedom of movement for persons, services and capital;

(d) the establishment of a common policy in the sphere of agriculture;

(e) the adoption of a common policy in the sphere of transport;

(f) the establishment of a system ensuring that competition in the common market is not distorted;

(g) the application of procedures by which the economic policies of Member States can be co-ordinated and disequilibria in their balances of payments can be remedied;

(h) the approximation of the laws of Member States to the extent required for proper functioning of the common market;

(i) the creation of a European Social Fund in order to improve the possibilities of employment for workers and to contribute to the raising of their standard of living;

(j) the establishment of a European Investment Bank to facilitate the economic expansion of the Community by opening up fresh resources; and

(k) the association of overseas countries and territories with a view to increasing trade and to promoting jointly economic and social development.

ARTICLE 4 (summary)

The tasks entrusted to the Community shall be carried out by the following institutions: a Parliamentary Assembly, a Council of Ministers, a Commission, a Court of Justice and an Economic and Social Committee which shall assist the Council and Commission in a consultative capacity.

ARTICLES 5 to 8 (summary)

Member states are required to ensure the carrying out of the Treaty obligations. Article 6 provides that member states 'shall, in close collaboration with the institutions of the Community co-ordinate their respective economic policies to the extent necessary to attain the objectives of this Treaty'. Community institutions must 'take care not to prejudice the internal and external financial stability of the member states'.

The Council may (under Article 7), on a proposal by the Commission and after consulting the Parliamentary Assembly, adopt, by a qualified majority, provisions designed to prohibit discrimination on the grounds of nationality within the field of application of this Treaty.

Article 8 sets out the conditions under which the Common Market was progressively established during a transitional period of 12 years, beginning in January 1958. [Note: The time-table for abolishing trade barriers between the Six was accelerated and completed by July 1, 1968.]

PART TWO—Foundations of the Community

TITLE I—FREE MOVEMENT OF GOODS

ARTICLE 9

1. The Community shall be based upon a customs union which shall cover all trade in goods and which shall involve the prohibition as between Member States of customs duties on imports and exports and of all taxes having equivalent effect, and the adoption of a common customs tariff in their relations with third countries.

2. The provisions of Chapter 1, Section 1 and Chapter 2 of this Title shall apply to the products originating in Member States and to products coming from third countries which are in free circulation in Member States. [Note: The term 'third country' which is frequently used in Community documents means a country which is not a member of the Common Market.]

ARTICLES 10, 11 (summary)

Products which come from a country outside the Common Market are considered to be in free circulation in a member state 'if the import formalities have been complied with, and any customs duties, or taxes having equivalent effect, which are payable have been levied in that member state, and if they have not benefited by a total or partial drawback of such duties or taxes'. Drawback is excise or import duty which is paid back when the goods on which it has been charged are exported.

CHAPTER 1—THE CUSTOMS UNION

SECTION 1
ELIMINATION OF CUSTOMS DUTIES AS BETWEEN MEMBER STATES

ARTICLE 12

Member States shall refrain from introducing, as between themselves, any new customs duties on imports or exports or any taxes having equivalent effect, and from increasing those which they already levy in their trade with each other.

ARTICLES 13 to 17 (summary)

These articles give the conditions under which customs duties between the Six have been eliminated. Changes in currency rates in the Six, however, have resulted in some border taxes for restricting the free flow of farm goods being temporarily reimposed in the early 1970s. The general rule is that a member state cannot, once the Common Market has been established, take unilateral action to reimpose restrictions on trade. A unanimous vote of the Council of Ministers is required under Article 235.

For customs duties designed essentially to produce revenue, the Six (under Article 17) retained the right to substitute internal taxes. These internal taxes must comply with Article 95 of the Treaty which requires that a member state 'must not impose, directly or indirectly, on the products of other member states any internal taxation of any kind in excess of that imposed directly or indirectly on similar domestic products'. There must be no taxation in one Market country which affords protection against goods from its partners.

Note: Under the British entry terms it was agreed that all industrial tariffs on trade between Britain and the Six should be eliminated in five equal stages, starting three months after accession.

The time-table below shows how the arrangements were due to work out on the assumption of British entry by January 1, 1973:

	Abolition of industrial tariffs between the Six and Britain (per cent)	Cumulative reduction (per cent)
APRIL 1, 1973	20	20
JANUARY 1, 1974	20	40
JANUARY 1, 1975	20	60
JANUARY 1, 1976	20	80
JULY 1, 1977	20	100

Therefore within three years of entry (when the Community's tariffs will have been cut by 80 per cent) British exporters will have almost duty-free access to the large market of the Six.

SECTION 2

SETTING UP OF THE COMMON CUSTOMS TARIFF

ARTICLE 18

The Member States declare their readiness to contribute to the development of international trade and the removal of obstacles thereto by entering into agreements, based on reciprocity and mutual advantage, whose object it shall be to reduce customs duties below the general level of which they could avail themselves as a result of the setting up of the customs union between them.

ARTICLES 19 to 29 (summary)

These articles provide for the setting up of the common external tariff (CET), the outer 'wall' of trade barriers placed around the Common Market of the Six towards the rest of the world. For the Six this 'wall' was calculated, apart from certain exceptions, on the arithmetical average of the customs duties applied by them on goods from the rest of the world on January 1, 1957. The CET was established on July 1, 1968, finally with the abolition of industrial customs duties charged between the Six.

Where a change in sources of supply or a shortage of supplies within the Community entails harmful consequences for the processing industries of a member state, the Commission can grant it tariff quotas at a reduced rate of duty or duty-free.

For certain products, listed in Annex II of the Treaty, the Commission may authorise any member state to suspend, in whole or in part, collection of the duties chargeable or may grant the state tariff quotas at a reduced rate of duty or duty-free, provided that no serious disturbance of the market of the products concerned results therefrom (Article 25).

Any independent alteration or suspension of duties in the common external tariff 'shall be decided by the Council unanimously' (Article 28).

In carrying out the tasks entrusted to it under this section the Commission shall be guided by the need to promote trade between the member states and the rest of the world and by:

'developments in conditions of competition within the Community in so far as they lead to an improvement in the competitive capacity of commercial concerns;

'the Community's requirements as regards the supply of raw materials and semi-finished goods; in this respect the Commission shall take care to avoid distorting, as between member states, conditions of competition in respect of finished goods;

'the need to avoid serious disturbances in the economies of member states and for ensuring rational development of production and an expansion of consumption within the Community.' (Article 29)

Note: Under the British entry terms, it was agreed that Britain should adjust its industrial tariffs on goods it imports from the rest of the world so as to align them with the common external tariff (CET) of the Six in four stages, beginning a year after accession. On the assumption of British entry by January 1, 1973, the following time-table for moving to the CET has been agreed:

	Adoption of the CET by Britain (per cent)	Cumulative movement towards adoption of CET (per cent)
1973	—	—
JANUARY 1, 1974	40	40
JANUARY 1, 1975	20	60
JANUARY 1, 1976	20	80
JULY 1, 1977	20	100

Britain under the entry terms is required, subject to certain special tariff arrangements, to apply the common external tariff to all countries neither belonging to, nor enjoying any special arrangements with, the enlarged Common Market. Countries expected to have special arrangements with the enlarged Market include those which are members of the European Free Trade Association (EFTA) but have not applied for entry into the Market, plus Britain's Commonwealth partners in Africa, the Caribbean, the Indian and Pacific Oceans, plus all its dependent territories (apart from Gibraltar and Hong Kong). Some 20 African countries which were formerly colonies of the Six also have special arrangements with the enlarged Market. The Market is also offering generalised preferences to developing countries.

For countries affected by CET *which at present have no preferential position in the British market, it will involve only fairly minor adjustments to the duties Britain applies to their goods; in general* CET *is rather lower than Britain's tariff. But for countries affected which have enjoyed free entry to the British market it will mean the gradual application of the* CET *to their exports to this country (e.g. Canada and Australia).*

SPECIAL TARIFF ARRANGEMENTS

Duties on most industrial raw materials are zero in the British tariff and CET, *but there are a number of items of particular importance to British industry which are dutiable under the* CET. *Britain's entry terms applying in this sector were designed to ensure that its membership in the Market would not lead to a new charge on supplies of these materials.*

In some cases it has been decided that the enlarged Common Market will be self-sufficient. For the rest, arrangements have been agreed with the Six which will ensure that about 90 per cent of our imports from outside the enlarged Market will continue to be imported free of duty. These arrangements will be helpful to Canada and Australia which are important suppliers of these materials.

The solutions agreed are as follows:

1. *For* woodpulp *and* lead bullion *(both key materials for industrial processing in the United Kingdom) the* CET *will either be completely suspended or equivalent arrangements made so that we are assured of continuing duty-free access to these products even beyond the end of the transitional period.*

2. *For* newsprint *we shall share in a Community duty-free quota up to the full extent of needs not covered by domestic production. This means that our newspaper publishers will be able to buy the balance of their requirements duty free from the sources they choose including both Canada and Scandinavia. Agreement was also reached on widening the definition of newsprint to include lighter weight newsprint: otherwise some of our newspapers who use this type of newsprint would have had to pay a* CET *of 12 per cent.*

3. *For* phosphorus *it has been agreed that we shall not start to apply the* CET *even at a reduced rate until 1977 and that it would be open to us then to apply for either suspension of the tariff or duty-free quotas.*

4. *For* alumina *it has been agreed that the* CET *would be suspended from its current level of 8·8 per cent to 5·5 per cent. Imports of alumina into the United Kingdom would be free of duty until January 1, 1976, would as from that date pay half the suspended rate, and would from July 1, 1977, pay the full 5·5 per cent rate. But it has been recognised that in the particular circumstances of the aluminium industry we should be able at any time after entry to apply in advance for a duty-free Community tariff quota for the period after January 1, 1976.*

5. *The remaining products on our list fall into two groups. For* plywood, *arrangements have been made, including a duty-free quota for certain specialised types of coniferous plywood which should continue to allow in most of our imports duty free. And for the* wattle extract *used by our tanners the* CET *will be cut by two-thirds, down to three per cent. These arrangements for plywood and wattle extract are not limited to the transitional period.*

6. *For the remaining products,* silicon carbide, ferro chrome, ferro silicon, refined lead *and* zinc *and* aluminium *it was established that we should be able to secure all or nearly all our needs duty free either from increased United Kingdom production or from other suppliers in the enlarged Community. And in the case of lead and zinc we shall be participating in existing Community tariff quotas which it has been agreed to adjust to take account of enlargement. Moreover in the case of certain of these products it has been agreed specifically that if the supply position were to change it would be open to us to apply for duty quotas.*

CHAPTER 2—ELIMINATION OF QUANTITATIVE RESTRICTIONS AS BETWEEN MEMBER STATES

ARTICLES 30 to 37 (summary)

Apart from certain minor exceptions, quantitative restrictions between the Six have been abolished under a time-table established on the basis of these Articles.

The Commission emphasised in the early 1970s the need to remove certain technical non-tariff barriers to trade which were being maintained in violation of Articles 30 to 32.

Article 36 provides that the provisions of Articles 30 to 34 shall not prevent the banning or restricting of imports, exports or goods in transit which are justified 'on the grounds of public morality; maintaining public order; public safety or security; the protection of health and life of humans, animals or plants; the protection of national treasures possessing artistic, historic or archaeological value; or the protection of industrial and commercial property'. These bans or restrictions must not 'amount to a means of arbitrary discrimination nor to a disguised restriction on trade between the member states'.

Article 37 provides for 'progressively adjusting' state trading monopolies so that there is no discrimination regarding supplies or marketing between the nationals of member states.

TITLE II—AGRICULTURE

ARTICLE 38

1. The common market shall extend to agriculture and trade in agricultural products. The term 'Agricultural products' shall mean the products of the soil, of stock-farming and of fisheries and products of first-stage processing directly related to the foregoing.

2. Except as otherwise provided in Articles 39 to 46 inclusive, the rules laid down for the establishment of the common market shall apply to agricultural products.

3. The products subject to the provisions of Articles 39 to 46 inclusive are listed in Annex II to this Treaty. Within a period of two years after this Treaty comes into force, however, the Council shall, by a qualified majority on a proposal from the Commission, decide what products should be added to this list.

4. The operation and development of the common market for agricultural products must be accompanied by the establishment of a common agricultural policy among the Member States.

ARTICLE 39

1. The objectives of the common agricultural policy shall be:

(*a*) to increase agricultural productivity by promoting technical progress and by ensuring the rational development of agricultural production and the optimum utilisation of all factors of production, in particular labour;

(*b*) thus to ensure a fair standard of living for the agricultural community, in particular by increasing the individual earnings of persons engaged in agriculture;

(*c*) to stabilise markets;

(*d*) to provide certainty of supplies;

(*e*) to ensure supplies to consumers at reasonable prices.

2. In working out the common agricultural policy, and any special methods which this may involve, account shall be taken of:

(*a*) the particular nature of agricultural activity, which results from agriculture's social structure and from structural and natural disparities between the various agricultural regions;

(*b*) the need to effect the appropriate adjustments by degrees;

(*c*) the fact that, in the Member States, agriculture constitutes a sector closely linked with the economy as a whole.

ARTICLE 40

1. Member States shall develop the common agricultural policy by degrees during the transitional period and shall bring it into force not later than at the end of that period.

2. In order to achieve the objectives set out in Article 39 a common organisation of agricultural markets shall be established.

This organisation shall take one of the following forms depending on the product concerned:

(*a*) common rules as regards competition;

(*b*) compulsory co-ordination of the various national marketing organisations; or

(*c*) a European organisation of the market.

3. The common organisation established in accordance with paragraph 2 of this Article may include all measures required to achieve the objectives set out in Article 39, in particular price controls, subsidies for the production and distribution of the various products, stock-piling and carry-over systems and common arrangements for stabilisation of imports or of exports.

The common organisation shall confine itself to pursuing the objectives set out in Article 39 and shall exclude any discrimination between producers or consumers within the Community.

Any common price policy shall be based on common criteria and uniform methods of calculation.

4. In order to enable the common organisation referred to in paragraph 2 of this Article to achieve its objectives, one or more agricultural orientation and guarantee funds may be set up.

ARTICLE 41

To enable the attainment of the objectives set out in Article 39, provision may in particular be made within the framework of the common agricultural policy for:

(a) an effective co-ordination of efforts in the spheres of vocational training, research in the science of agriculture and the dissemination of knowledge relating thereto; this may include jointly financed projects or institutions;

(b) joint measures to develop the consumption of certain products.

ARTICLE 42

The provisions of the chapter dealing with the rules of competition shall only apply to the production of, and trade in, agricultural products, to the extent determined by the Council within the framework of Articles 43 (2) and (3) and in accordance with the procedure laid down therein, account being taken of the objectives defined in Article 39.

The Council may, in particular, authorise the grant of aid:

(a) for the protection of undertakings handicapped by structural or natural conditions;

(b) within the framework of economic development programmes.

ARTICLE 43 (summary)

This sets out the procedural and other steps which the Six took to create the common agricultural policy (CAP) and to form the common agricultural market.

ARTICLE 44

1. During the transitional period and in so far as progressive abolition of customs duties and quantitative restrictions between Member States may result in prices likely to jeopardise the achievement of the objectives set out in Article 39, each Member State shall be entitled to apply to particular products, in a non-discriminatory manner and in substitution for quotas, and to such an extent as shall not impede the expansion of the volume of trade provided for in Article 45 (2), a system of minimum prices below which imports may be:

—temporarily suspended or reduced; or
—allowed, but at a price higher than the minimum price fixed for the product concerned.

In the second event the minimum prices shall not include customs duties.

2. Minimum prices shall not be such as to cause a reduction of the trade existing between Member States when this Treaty comes into force nor such as to obstruct a progressive expansion of this trade. Minimum prices shall not be applied so as to form an obstacle to the development of a natural preference between Member States.

3. As soon as this Treaty comes into force the Council shall, on a proposal from the Commission, determine objective criteria for the establishment of minimum price systems and for the fixing of such prices.

These criteria shall in particular take account of the average national cost prices in the Member State applying the minimum price, of the position of the various undertakings concerned in relation to such average cost prices, and of the need to promote both a progressive improvement of agricultural operations and adjustments and specialisation needed within the common market.

The Commission shall further propose a procedure for revising these criteria, so as to take account of and accelerate technical progress and for progressively approximating prices within the common market.

These criteria and the procedure for revising them shall be unanimously determined by the Council within three years of this Treaty's coming into force.

4. Until the Council's decision takes effect, Member States may fix minimum prices on condition that they first communicate them to the Commission and to the other Member States so as to enable them to submit their comments.

As soon as the Council has taken its decision, Member States shall fix minimum prices based on the criteria determined as above.

The Council may, by a qualified majority on a proposal from the Commission, rectify any decisions taken by Member States which do not conform with the criteria defined above.

5. With effect from the beginning of the third stage and should it not have proved possible to settle the aforementioned objective criteria for certain products, the Council may, by a qualified majority, on a proposal from the Commission, vary the minimum prices in force in respect of such products.

6. When the transitional period ends, a table of minimum prices still in force shall be drawn up. The Council, acting on a proposal from the Commission and by a majority of nine votes, in accordance with the weighting provided for in Article 148 (2), first paragraph, shall determine the system to be applied within the framework of the common agricultural policy.

ARTICLE 45

1. Until replacement of national organisations by one of the forms of common organisation referred to in Article 40 (2), for products in respect of which there exist in certain Member States:

— arrangements designed to guarantee to national producers a market for their products, and
— import requirements,

the development of trade shall be effected by the conclusion of agreements or long-term contracts between Member States and the exporting countries.

These agreements or contracts shall be directed towards the progressive abolition of any discrimination in the application of these arrangements to the various producers within the Community.

The conclusion of such agreements or contracts shall take place during the first stage; the principle of reciprocity shall be taken into account.

2. As regards prices, these agreements or contracts shall be based on the average volume of trade between Member States in the products concerned during the three years before this Treaty comes into force, and shall provide for an increase in the volume of trade within the limits of existing requirements, taking account of traditional patterns of trade.

As regards prices, these agreements or contracts shall enable producers to dispose of the agreed quantities at prices which shall be progressively approximated to those paid to national producers in the purchasing country's domestic market.

This approximation shall be effected as smoothly as possible and shall be completed not later than the end of the transitional period.

Prices shall be negotiated between the parties concerned within the framework of directives drawn up by the Commission for the purpose of implementing the immediately preceding two sub-paragraphs.

If the first stage is extended, these agreements or contracts shall continue to be carried out under the conditions applying at the end of the fourth year after this Treaty comes into force, the obligations to increase quantities and to approximate prices being suspended until the second stage begins.

Member States shall avail themselves of any opportunity open to them under their legislation, particularly in respect of import policy, to ensure the conclusion and carrying out of these agreements or contracts.

3. To the extent that Member States require raw materials for the production of goods intended for export outside the Community in competition with producers in third countries, the above agreements or contracts shall not impede the importation of raw materials intended for this purpose from third countries. This provision shall not, however, apply if the Council unanimously decides to supply the sums needed to make good the difference between the higher price incurred in respect of importation for this purpose on the basis of these agreements or contracts and the delivery prices of the same goods purchased on the world market.

ARTICLE 46

Where in a Member State a product is subjected to a national marketing organisation or to some internal rules to a like effect, which affect the competitive position of a like sphere of production in another Member State, a countervailing duty on importation shall be applied by Member States to this product where it comes from the Member State where the organisation or rules exist, unless that State applies a countervailing duty on export.

The Commission shall fix the amount of such duties at the level necessary to redress the balance; it may also authorise recourse to other measures, the conditions and details of which it shall determine.

ARTICLE 47

As to the functions to be performed by the Economic and Social Committee in the application of this Title, its agricultural section shall have as task that of holding itself at the service of the Commission for the purpose of preparing the conclusions of the Committee in accordance with the provisions of Articles 197 and 198.

Note: Under its entry terms Britain agreed to adopt the common agricultural policy. This maintains the level of market prices for the main agricultural commodities in two ways: the price of imports is kept up to a minimum or threshold price by means of variable import levies; and the internal market is supported at an intervention price slightly below the threshold price, at which any surplus is bought by the Community's Agricultural Fund.

These arrangements apply to cereals, milk products, beef and veal, pigmeat (i.e. pork, ham and bacon) and sugar, and (except for support-buying) to poultry and eggs, and horticulture though they vary for each. The Agricultural Fund also compensates Community exporters when their sales to countries outside the Common Market are made at prices below Community levels.

In the first year of British entry (expected to be on January 1, 1973), Britain will apply this Community system of support, though not Community prices. It will introduce threshold and intervention prices of its own. These will be lower than the full Community threshold and intervention prices, the difference corresponding to the difference between our British market price levels and those of the Six. Britain will then increase its threshold and intervention prices gradually to full Community levels by six steps over a period of five years (known as the transitional period). These will be equal steps, subject to a 10 per cent tolerance up or down if needed in the interests of flexibility. As market food prices in Britain are brought up to the higher levels now existing in the Six, British farmers will increasingly get their returns from the Market, and the deficiency payments system will be phased out.

There will be free trade with the Six in the products concerned, subject only, throughout the transitional period, to arrangements to compensate for the differences in price levels. These will take the form of fixed levies on British exports to the Six and fixed compensatory payments on return exports. These levies and export payments will be gradually reduced by six steps over the five years, as prices come into line. There will be comparable arrangements for trade between the Six and the other countries applying for membership, Ireland, Denmark and Norway, and between the applicant countries.

The levy system will give products in the enlarged Common Market preference over imports from other countries whenever market prices are below the threshold. British farmers will share in this preference throughout the Common Market and will have the safeguard of the intervention prices to support their market.

For those agricultural commodities for which the Community has a common external tariff instead of, or in addition to, levies, the transitional arrangements will take the form of tariff adjustments similar to those agreed for industrial goods (see note following summary of Articles 15 to 17). Similarly, the British tariff on these commodities will be adjusted to the CET.

For horticulture, *which depends on the tariff as its main form of protection, there will be a slower rate of tariff adjustment with no change at all in the first year of transition (planned for 1973). For apples and pears our existing import quotas will be replaced by compensatory import levies offsetting the difference between British and Community prices. These levies will be phased out over five years to bring prices gradually into line, with the same provision for flexibility as in the case of agricultural prices.*

It was agreed as part of the British entry terms that the enlarged Common Market will be ready to take prompt and effective action to remedy any difficulties arising out of the transitional arrangements for British agriculture and horticulture or any threat of abrupt dislocation to Commonwealth and other suppliers which are not members or associates of the Common Market.

The Six agreed just as the negotiations on British entry were beginning in June, 1970, to apply a Common Fisheries Policy *allowing free access for their fishing vessels in each other's coastal waters. Under this policy there would be common rules for marketing fish throughout the member states. Britain and the other applicants asked for changes in the common policy to safeguard special interests.*

TITLE III—THE FREE MOVEMENT OF PERSONS, SERVICES AND CAPITAL
CHAPTER 1—WORKERS

ARTICLES 48 to 51 (summary)

Workers who are citizens of any one member state in the Common Market can, under regulations which have been applied on the basis of these articles, take jobs in any of the other member states with the same rights as nationals of those states. In other words member states may no longer, apart from employment in the public service, discriminate against a Community national by giving priority in employment or placement to their own citizens.

This free movement of labour means that workers in one Market country not only have the right to take paid employment in any of the others but they can go to any of them for three months to look for work there. They are no longer required by the authorities of the other member states to have work permits, but still require residence permits. Residence permits are issued for five years automatically renewable unless work period is under one year. They may be refused for reasons concerned with maintaining public order, security or health.

Workers in member states, seeking jobs in the others, enjoy 'Community priority' over the nationals of non-member countries. Nationals of member states, working in the others, receive equal treatment in every important field relating to employment. This includes taxation, social insurance, the right to send for members of their families and dependents, the right to rent or own a house, and the right to be elected to workers' representative bodies at the place of employment.

Note: The British entry terms allow free movement of labour between Britain and all the other nine members of the enlarged Common Market as from January 1, 1973. Certain exceptions are being considered which would restrict the movement from Britain to the Continent of immigrants seeking jobs who have only recently arrived in Britain (see Chapter 17, p. 166).

It was also agreed that the free movement of labour rules would not be applied for the present to Northern Ireland. Any available work there should, it was agreed, be reserved for residents of Northern Ireland in the first instance.

CHAPTER 2—THE RIGHT OF ESTABLISHMENT

ARTICLES 52 to 58 (summary)

Freedom of establishment, i.e. freedom to set up in business or in practice, is provided for nationals of any member state in any of the others.

The ultimate aim is that firms, branches, agencies and individuals, such as bankers, insurance brokers and wholesale and retail distributors, would be given the right to establish themselves freely in any of the member states.

CHAPTER 3—SERVICES

ARTICLES 59 to 66 (summary)

Restrictions on freedom to provide services within the Community from one state to another are being progressively abolished. 'Services' include in particular those provided by occupations of an industrial or commercial character, occupations in small craft industries and professional occupations.

The liberalisation of banking and insurance services would be done 'in step with the liberalisation of movement of capital'.

Decisions for implementing these articles were delayed in the 1960s because of difficulty in agreeing on the equivalence of qualifications in the various professions in member states. Countries are not pledged to adopt identical legislation and regulations but are asked to ensure that nationals of other Community countries enjoy the same rights as their own citizens.

By the early 1970s the Six had removed restrictions against nationals of other member states in oil exploration, reinsurance, real estate, mining, gas and electricity production and some aspects of agriculture and forestry.

The Commission submitted proposals for lawyers, veterinarians, nurses, midwives, opticians, dentists, pharmacists, doctors, engineers, insurance agents, bankers, architects, accountants, surveyors, journalists, sports instructors, road and inland waterway hauliers and travelling salesmen.

CHAPTER 4—CAPITAL

ARTICLES 67 to 73 (summary)

Application of these Articles in the Six removes restrictions on movements of capital between member states 'to the extent necessary to ensure the proper functioning of the Common Market' (Article 67).

There should be 'progressive co-ordination of the exchange policies of the member states in respect of movement of capital between those States and non-member countries' (Article 70). They should endeavour 'to achieve the highest possible degree of liberalisation'.

Member states are required to keep the Commission informed of any known movements of capital to and from non-member countries and the Commission 'may deliver opinions on this subject' (Article 72).

The Commission can authorise a member state to take protective measures in the field of those capital movements which lead to a disturbance in the operation of that state's capital market. The state which is in difficulties 'may, however, itself take the measures mentioned above on grounds of secrecy or urgency, should such measures prove necessary'. It should 'inform the Commission of such measures not later than the date when they come into force'. The Commission may, after the Monetary Committee has been consulted, decide that the state concerned shall amend or abolish such measures (Article 73).

Note: Britain, as part of the entry terms, was given a five-year transitional period to free capital movements between it and the Community. The following time-table was laid down: Direct investment: *There will be a substantial interim relaxation on the date of entry (expected to be January 1, 1973), and full conformity by the end of the second year, when residents in Britain will be able to obtain foreign exchange at the official rate of exchange for direct investment in the European Economic Community.*

Personal capital movements: *For residents in Britain who take up employment in the other Market member states there will be free movement of capital from the start. For other movements of a personal nature (e.g. buying a house to retire in a Common Market country) there will be liberalisation within about two and a half years.*

Portfolio investment: *There will be a freeing of movement towards the end of the transitional period.*

Acceleration: *This time-table is aimed at securing even phasing. But Britain agrees that it may be possible to accelerate it in the light of developments and experience during the transitional period.*

TITLE IV—TRANSPORT

ARTICLES 74 to 84 (summary)

Only limited progress had been made by the Six until the 1970s to implement a common transport policy called for in these Articles. Common policies were agreed upon in some sectors for road, rail and inland waterway transport of passengers and freight. Air and sea transport were excluded at first but the Commission has called for common policies covering airlines and cargo ships.

The aims of Community transport policy are to ensure that its transport system meets the needs of expanding internal trade; and that conditions of competition are as harmonised as possible, between different types of transport and between the transport networks of the member states.

A system of what are called 'forked tariffs' was brought into force in 1969 for road haulage. The tariffs were defined by an upper and lower limit and were applied to carriers at the frontiers of the Six. A Community quota system for road haulage between member states in which 1,200 licences are divided among the Six is being tried out. The basis for deciding which state subsidies for rail, road and inland waterway transport are authorised was laid down in a 1970 regulation. It was also agreed to standardise the accounts of the railways of the Six. As a step towards complete harmony of competition between haulage firms in the member states they agreed on common rules for drivers of passenger and goods vehicles. These limit driving hours to eight hours a day and provide that trucks and coaches must carry a monitoring 'box'.

PART THREE—Policy of the Community

TITLE I—COMMON RULES

CHAPTER 1—RULES OF COMPETITION

SECTION 1

RULES APPLYING TO UNDERTAKINGS

ARTICLES 85 to 90 (summary)

These prohibit all agreements or concerted practices entered into by firms which restrain trade between member states by distorting competition. In particular, the rules prohibit such agreements or practices involving price-fixing, market-sharing, restriction of production or technical development and discriminatory supply conditions.

The Commission is given special powers of supervision. Agreements, it says, are authorised where the overall economic effects are likely to be beneficial by improving production and distribution or by technical progress or where the restraint on competition or trade is negligible.

The first regulation made in this field, in 1962, provided that agreements could be automatically banned in the absence of special authorisation and required firms to register, with the Commission, agreements between two or more of them which are liable to affect trade between member states. The Commission has the right to approve or ban the agreement or ask the firms to modify it. Under the regulation the Commission may impose heavy fines for infringements of the fair competition rules and has important powers of inspection and control.

Decisions by the Commission and the European Court of Justice have laid the basis of case law for deciding whether certain kinds of agreements between firms are permissible. The rules, the Commission emphasises, do not affect competition within a member state. They are intended to ensure that firms do not deprive customers of the benefits of economic integration by creating cross-frontier cartels.

By the 1970s over 40-thousand agreements had been declared permissible by the Commission. Of these, the largest group is that under which a manufacturer can grant exclusive dealing rights. These 'are allowed if, for example, they are of a purely regional character within a single country and only indirectly affect imports or exports'. In a statement published in 1970, the Commission said an agreement should be notified only if 'it has an appreciable effect on trade with the Community . . . that is, if it covers more than five per cent of the market and if the annual turnover of firms involved exceeds 15-million dollars or 20-million for certain groups of firms'.

The Commission has imposed fines on groups of firms producing dyestuffs and quinine and these have been challenged in the European Court.

Under Article 86 the Commission can act to prevent monopolies. In the first case in this category the Commission accused an American company of 'exploiting its dominant position in the market' by taking over two of Europe's large can makers and merging them.

SECTION 2

DUMPING PRACTICES

ARTICLE 91 (summary)

The Common Market has a common policy covering dumping practices based on the anti-dumping code of the General Agreement on Tariffs and Trade (GATT). Dumping occurs when goods are sold abroad at prices below those in the exporter's home market.

Note: During entry negotiations Britain received clarification of the likely effects of the Market's anti-dumping rules.

SECTION 3

AIDS GRANTED BY STATES

ARTICLES 92 to 94 (summary)

Apart from help for disaster areas or for underdeveloped regions, aid granted by a member state or through state resources which distorts, or threatens to distort, competition by favouring certain firms, or the production of certain goods, is declared under Article 92 'incompatible with the Common Market'. The Commission may bring a state which infringes this rule before the European Court of Justice.

CHAPTER 2—TAX PROVISIONS

ARTICLES 95 to 99 (summary)

To conform with the requirements set out in these, the Six agreed that by 1972 a single uniform system of turnover tax, the value-added tax (VAT), would be applied throughout the Common Market. Agreement to standardise VAT rates of the member states was expected later. Goods will then be traded in across their common frontiers without being subject to refunds and taxes.

Note: VAT *will be introduced in Britain in 1973.*

The Commission is also urging the alignment of member states' company taxes to encourage cross-frontier mergers and the removal of double taxation of dividends and interest. For tourists there are now common rules on how much tobacco, wine and spirits can be taken duty-free from one state to another. Taxes on the raising of capital had largely been harmonised by 1969. Immediate harmonising of income tax is not planned because it does not directly influence the functioning of the Common Market.

CHAPTER 3—APPROXIMATION OF LAWS

ARTICLES 100 to 102 (summary)

National laws and administrative provisions directly affecting the running of the Common Market must, under these articles, be harmonised, since differences between them hamper the Market. Article 101 authorises the Commission to consult member states where a discrepancy between laws interferes with fair competition in the Market.

These Articles are the basis for steps taken to harmonise the system by which public works contracts are awarded in the member countries, and for the creation of a European company statute, a Community patent law and agreements for mutual recognition of each other's professional and educational diplomas.

TITLE II—ECONOMIC POLICY

CHAPTER 1—POLICY ON CURRENT TRENDS

ARTICLE 103 (summary)

Member states agree that they should regard their policy on current economic trends as a matter of common concern and should consult each other and the Commission on measures which may have to be taken.

CHAPTER 2—BALANCE OF PAYMENTS

ARTICLES 104 to 109 (summary)

Each member state agrees under Article 104 to 'pursue the economic policy necessary to ensure the equilibrium of its overall balance of payments and to maintain confidence in its currency, a high level of employment and stable price levels'. To achieve this they agree to co-ordinate their economic policies by collaboration between administrative departments and between central banks (Article 105). A Monetary Committee to keep under review the monetary, financial and general payments situations of the member states has since been created.

A five-year medium-term economic plan covering the period 1971–5 was drawn up by the Commission to help economic co-ordination. It covers unemployment, price inflation, growth rate and balance of payments. In 1970 the Six agreed to set up a 2,000-million dollar reserves pool to provide short-term monetary help to a member state in balance of payments difficulties.

Each member state is required to treat its policy on exchange rates as a matter of common interest (Article 107). If a member alters its exchange rate in a way which conflicts with Article 104 and seriously distorts competition the Commission may authorise other members to take necessary steps to deal with the consequences.

The Commission may (Article 108) recommend that a state take certain measures to deal with serious balance of payments and currency difficulties if they are upsetting the Common Market. In certain circumstances the Commission can authorise a state in difficulties to take protective measures. These can be changed by the Council.

When a sudden crisis in the balance of payments occurs and if a decision under Article 108 is not taken immediately, the member state concerned 'may provisionally take the necessary protective measures' (Article 109). These must cause the least possible disturbance to the Common Market and must not be wider in scope than is needed to deal with the crisis. The Commission and other members must be told of the protective measures 'not later than when they come into force'. The Council 'may decide, by a qualified majority, that the state concerned shall amend, suspend or abolish the protective measures'.

CHAPTER 3—COMMERCIAL POLICY

ARTICLES 110 to 116 (summary)

The external trade policy of the Common Market (called the common commercial policy) is to be conducted by the Commission. Its greatest achievement in this field was acting on behalf of the Six in the Kennedy Round worldwide tariff cutting negotiations.

Common rules have been agreed for a large part of the Community's imports of agricultural goods not subject to the common farm policy and all manufactured goods imported from non-Communist countries (about 90 per cent of the Community's foreign trade). Common rules for trade with state-trading countries (mainly the Soviet Union and Eastern Europe) were adopted by the Six in December, 1969. Until the end of 1972, however, a member state is allowed to make bilateral agreements with certain state-trading countries, particularly those in Eastern Europe which have so far refused to negotiate with or recognise the Common Market as a unit. Member states must nevertheless obtain approval of Community institutions before beginning negotiations and before concluding an agreement. After January 1, 1973, all trade negotiations with countries outside the Market will have to be conducted by the Commission on behalf of all member states.

TITLE III—SOCIAL POLICY

CHAPTER 1—SOCIAL PROVISIONS

ARTICLE 117

Member States agree upon the need to promote better conditions of living and of work and employment for workers, so as to lead to their progressive harmonisation and improvement.

They believe that such a development will ensue not only from the operation of the common market, which will favour the harmonisation of social systems, but also from the procedures provided for in this Treaty and from the approximation of provisions imposed by law, regulation and administrative action.

ARTICLES 118 to 122 (summary)

The Commission is required by Article 118 to promote the close collaboration between member states in the social field, particularly in matters related to employment, labour law and working conditions, basic and advanced vocational training, social security, protection against occupational accidents and diseases, occupational hygiene, the laws of trade unions, and collective bargaining between employers and workers.

In the early 1970s the Six agreed to try and harmonise social security policies, and to move towards co-ordinating social policies in other fields. A standing Committee on Employment has been formed to give trade unions and management a voice in policies related to employment at a Community level.

Under Article 119 member states must follow a common policy of 'equal remuneration for the same work between male and female workers'. The Six have been slow to act on the Commission's request to meet the requirements of this article in full.

CHAPTER 2—THE EUROPEAN SOCIAL FUND

ARTICLES 123 to 128 (summary)

On the basis of these, a European Social Fund has been established to help ensure the re-employment of workers who have to change their jobs in member states as a result of technological developments in industry and the effects of economic integration and greater competition.

The Fund repays the member states up to half of their expenditure on vocational retraining or redeployment of workers. Unions and management are consulted. It can aid private as well as public undertakings and workers from non-member as well as member countries.

Payments from the Fund came from the Community's budget.

TITLE IV—THE EUROPEAN INVESTMENT BANK

ARTICLES 129 and 130 (summary)

The European Investment Bank, set up under these Articles, grants loans and guarantees on a non-profitmaking basis for less developed regions, modernisation schemes in member states and projects of common interest to some of them. It has financed such things as road building and construction of factories. By the end of 1970 the Bank had approved more than three-hundred loans and guarantees totalling nearly 2,000-million dollars and had raised more than 1,000-million dollars on international capital markets to help finance these operations. A special section of the Bank helps African and other associate members of the Market and member states' dependencies.

Note: Britain has agreed to contribute the same subscription to the capital of the Bank as France and West Germany (£187·5-million of which £37·5-million will be paid up). Most of Britain's contribution is expected to remain in this country. Britain also agreed to contribute £24-million to the Bank's reserves under similar conditions. It will be represented in the Bank's management on the same footing as France, West Germany and Italy.

PART FOUR—Association of the Overseas Countries and Territories

ARTICLES 131 to 136 (summary)

Former colonies and territories of France, Belgium, the Netherlands and Italy in Africa and elsewhere are linked to the Common Market 'to promote their economic and social development . . . in accordance with the principles stated in the Preamble to this Treaty . . . in such manner as to lead them to the economic, social and cultural development to which they aspire'.

Eighteen states (17 African plus Malagasay) are signatories of the Yaoundé Convention which extends until January 31, 1975. They are: *Gabon, Zaire, Congo-Brazzaville, Cameroon, Upper Volta, Ivory Coast, Somalia, Niger, Senegal, Chad, Burundi, Mali, Dahomey, Central African Republic, Rwanda, Togo, Mauritania,* and *Malagasay.*

Most of the products of these associated states of the Common Market (referred to as associated overseas territories or AOTs) entered the Common Market duty-free since July 1, 1968. Agricultural products imported by Market member states are handled on a case-by-case basis but are given preference over countries which are not associates under Part Four. The associate states, in return, began reducing their tariffs on imports from Market states and abolishing quota restrictions. The AOTs were however allowed to keep duties on goods from the Six to protect their infant industries. The Six agreed that the AOTs could participate in a system of generalised tariff preferences initiated in the United Nations.

Under the Yaoundé Convention a European Development Fund has been set up with 1,000-million dollars of resources.

Three African members of the Commonwealth have, under the Arusha Convention, which runs until January 31, 1975, become associates of the Market. They are: *Kenya, Uganda* and *Tanzania. (Nigeria* signed an association agreement in 1966 but, as it was not ratified, it lapsed.) They have duty-free entry into the Common Market for many of their products, except that quotas were at first applied to coffee, cloves and canned pineapple. The Six agreed to consider their interests in developing its common agricultural policy. In return the three African Commonwealth countries agreed to grant tariff concessions on sixty products of the Six.

Association agreements between the Common Market and the overseas countries under Part Four are supervised through a joint Association Council and a joint Parliamentary Committee.

Note: Under arrangements negotiated between Britain and the Six, all the independent Commonwealth countries in Africa, the Caribbean, the Indian Ocean *and* Pacific Ocean *can become associate members of the Common Market. Association was also offered to* all British dependent territories (*and the Anglo-French condominium of the* New Hebrides *under Part Four, with the exception of Gibraltar and Hong Kong.* Gibraltar *was covered by Article 227 (4) of the Rome Treaty but is not in the customs territory of the enlarged Market.* Hong Kong *was included in the Common Market's scheme of generalised preferences.* Malta *had an association agreement with the Market, including preferential trading arrangements, in 1971 and there were arrangements for associating with* Cyprus *and* Mauritius.

The Six agreed to make special arrangements for linking the Channel Islands *and* Isle of Man *with the enlarged Common Market.*

PART FIVE—The Community's Institutions

TITLE I—INSTITUTIONAL PROVISIONS

CHAPTER 1—INSTITUTIONS

SECTION 1

THE ASSEMBLY

ARTICLES 137 to 144 (summary)

The Assembly, also called the European Parliament, 'shall exercise the advisory and supervisory powers conferred on it by this Treaty' (Article 137).

It consists of delegates nominated by the respective legislatures from the member states. The European Parliament has its headquarters in Luxembourg and meets in Strasbourg.

Note: It was agreed under the entry terms that the number of members will be as follows: Britain 36; France 36; Germany 36; Italy 36; Netherlands 14; Belgium 14; Denmark 10; Ireland 10; Norway 10; Luxembourg 6.

Article 138 provides that the Assembly shall draw up proposals for elections by direct universal suffrage in accordance with a uniform procedure in all member states. The Council of Ministers of the Market 'shall unanimously decide on the provisions to be recommended to member states for adoption in accordance with their respective constitutional rules'.

Members of the Commission can attend all Assembly meetings and address it on behalf of the Commission. It is required to reply orally or in writing to questions from members. It has the power, under Article 144 to dismiss the Commission by a two-thirds majority of the votes cast if that constitutes a majority of the members.

The Six agreed to allow the Assembly to exercise very limited power over a sector of the Common budget.

Note: Britain has informed the Six that it is prepared to consider suggestions for strengthening the Assembly.

SECTION 2

THE COUNCIL

ARTICLES 145 to 154 (summary)

To achieve the objects of the Treaty the Council 'shall ensure co-ordination of the general economic policies of the member states' and 'have power to take decisions' (Article 145). Each national government is represented on the Council by a minister. The presidency of the Council is occupied for a six-month period by each member in rotation according to the alphabetical order of the member states (Article 146).

Article 148 says that, except where otherwise provided for in the Treaty, the Council's decisions shall be by a majority of its members. As has been explained, however, in the chapters on what the Market is and how it works the Community practice is to proceed only by unanimity when member states' vital interests are at issue.

Note: It was agreed in the entry negotiations that, where qualified majority with weighting of votes is provided for, the votes of the Council of an enlarged Community would have the following weighting: Britain 10; France 10; Italy 10; Germany 10; Belgium 5; Netherlands 5; Denmark 3; Ireland 3; Norway 3; Luxembourg 2.

When the Council decision by qualified majority is required following a Commission proposal, it can only be effective if at least 43 of the 61 votes are cast in favour.

In some cases, the Treaty provides that voting shall take place by qualified majority without a Commission proposal. In these cases, decisions are approved only if 43 votes or more are cast in favour by at least six member states. In those cases where a simple majority is provided for, the majority will, of course, be six out of the ten states.

The Council can only amend a proposal, put before it by the Commission, by unanimous decision. So long as the Council has not taken a decision, the Commission may amend its original proposal, in particular when the Assembly has been consulted on that proposal.

SECTION 3

THE COMMISSION

ARTICLES 155 to 163 (summary)

To ensure the working and development of the Common Market, the Commission sees that all provisions of this Treaty and measures taken by its institutions are carried out. It makes recommendations or gives opinions on matters dealt with in the Treaty if it expressly provides for them, or if the Commission thinks it necessary. It has its own power of decision and moulds policies for submission to the Council. Finally the Commission exercises powers conferred on it by the Council to ensure implementation of Council rules.

ARTICLE 157. Only nationals of member states may be members of the Commission.

The Commission may not include more than two members having the nationality of the same state.

The members of the Commission shall be completely independent in the performance of their functions, in the general interest of the Community.

In the performance of their duties, they shall neither seek nor take instructions from any Government or from any other body. They shall refrain from any action incompatible with the character of their functions. Each member state undertakes to respect this principle and not to seek to influence the members of the Commission in the performance of their task.

The members of the Commission may not, during their term of office, engage in any other paid or unpaid occupation. When entering upon their duties they shall give a solemn undertaking that, both during and after their term of office, they will respect the obligations arising therefrom and in particular their duty to exercise honesty and discretion as regards the acceptance, after they have ceased to hold office, of certain appointments or benefits. In the event of any breach of these obligations, the Court of Justice, on the application of the Council or of the Commission, may, according to the circumstances, rule that the member concerned either be compulsorily retired in accordance with the provisions of Article 160 or forfeit his right to a pension or other benefits in lieu thereof.

Note: In an enlarged Common Market the Commission, which in 1971 consisted of nine members, would be increased to 14, two each from Britain, France, Germany and Italy, and one from each of the other states.

SECTION 4

THE COURT OF JUSTICE

ARTICLES 164 to 188 (summary)

The Court of Justice ensures that the law is observed in the interpretation and implementation of the Rome, Euratom and Paris Treaties. Britain and the other applicants would be entitled to appoint judges to the Court and probably an advocate general. For the Community of the Six it had seven judges and two advocates general. These posts must be chosen from persons whose impartiality is beyond question and who are qualified to hold the highest judicial office in their respective countries or who are lawyers of the highest standing.

The Court's jurisdiction falls into three main categories:

1. Jurisdiction in proceedings brought against a member state by the Commission or by another member state for a breach of its obligations under the three Community Treaties. The Court's judgment establishes the breach, but does not impose legal sanctions against the offending state. Defaulting states are relied upon to remedy any breach of their obligations found by the Court.

2. Supervising the way the Community institutions exercise their powers in cases, not only brought against member states or by other Community institutions, in those brought by firms or individuals challenging the acts of the institutions, appealing against penalties or claiming damages.

3. Jurisdiction to rule on questions arising in national courts and tribunals on the interpretations of the provisions of the Treaties. Most of the Court's cases are in this category. It can also rule on questions arising in national courts and tribunals on the validity of the instruments made under the Treaties. National courts refer such questions to the European Court.

Judgments of the European Court and decisions of the Brussels Commission imposing sanctions on individuals and firms are enforced by national courts.

By 1970, more than seven-hundred cases had been submitted to the Court. Of these, it gave judgment in 518 of them and 120 were settled at an earlier stage.

CHAPTER 2—PROVISIONS COMMON TO SEVERAL INSTITUTIONS

ARTICLES 189 to 192 (summary)

The Council of Ministers and the Commission carry out their task under the Treaty by making regulations, issuing directives, taking decisions, making recommendations or giving opinions (Article 189).

Regulations apply generally. They are binding in their entirety and take 'direct effect in each member state'.

Directives are binding as to the result to be achieved upon each member state to which they are directed, while leaving to national authorities the choice of form and methods.

Decisions are binding in their entirety upon those to whom they are directed.

Recommendations and *opinions* have no binding force.

Regulations, directives and decisions 'shall be fully reasoned' (Article 190). Regulations are published in the Community's Official Journal and take effect either on a date provided for or, failing this, on the twentieth day after publication.

Directives and decisions are notified to those to whom they are directed and shall take effect on notification (Article 191).

Decisions of the Council or of the Commission which involve a money obligation on persons other than states, shall have the weight of a Court Judgment. Article 192, which establishes this, sets out the procedure followed by member states in enforcing the decisions under their own operational rules.

CHAPTER 3—THE ECONOMIC AND SOCIAL COMMITTEE

ARTICLES 193 to 198 (summary)

An Economic and Social Committee has been formed with consultative status, consisting of representatives of employers, trade unions, producers, farmers, carriers, dealers, small craft industries, professional occupations and 'representatives of the general interest'. The Committee must be consulted by the Council or Commission where the Treaty so provides before policy or certain other decisions are taken.

Note: Britain, as a member, would have 24 representatives on the Committee, the equivalent of France, Germany and Italy.

TITLE II—FINANCIAL PROVISIONS

ARTICLES 199 to 208 (summary)

A Community budget has been established on the basis of these articles. Most of its funds have been used to pay for the common agriculural policy including the cost of supporting farm prices, improvement schemes, export refunds and payments to encourage farmers to leave the land.

The rest of the funds covered administrative costs of the Community institutions, the European Social Fund, Euratom and food aid.

The common budget system came into force on January 1, 1971. It was agreed by the Six that, over the subsequent seven years, the Community would phase in a system under which its budget would be provided with automatic payments ('own resources'). They consist of the revenues from import levies on farm imports, customs duties on imports of industrial goods and part of the VAT (value-added tax). From 1978 the Community will be financially autonomous.

It was agreed to apply the system in two phases:

From 1971 to 1974 the budget would consist of, first, the levies collected on agricultural imports (less ten per cent returned to the member states to cover the cost of collection); second, an annually increasing proportion of the revenue from customs duties on other imports, beginning with up to half of the total levies and duties (less ten per cent returned for administrative costs); third, direct contributions from member states, according to an agreed 'key' (related to the gross national product, GNP of each member state to cover any shortfall).

From 1975 the budget will consist of all the levies and customs duties (less ten per cent for administration) and the revenue of up to a one per cent rate of value-added tax.

What are called 'correctives' are applied to prevent a sharp increase or decrease in the payments into the budget in any one year. From 1971 to 1974 these correctives ensure that they do not rise by more than one per cent or fall by more than one and a half per cent from the previous year. From 1975 to the end of 1977 the payments must not rise or fall by more than two per cent.

Note: Under the British entry terms it was agreed that Britain would phase in its financial contributions to the common budget over a five-year period beginning in 1973. It would pay 8·64 per cent of the budget in that year, rising to 18·92 per cent in 1977. Assuming that the common budget amounts to £1,400-million in 1973 and rises to £1,600-million by 1977, Britain's net contribution (after allowing for certain receipts it would have from the budget) is estimated at £100-million in 1973 rising to £200-million in 1977. By the 1980s much more of the common budget money is due to be spent on non-agricultural activities such as industrial and regional development, in which case Britain could expect to enjoy much larger receipts. These, it is estimated, would prevent a sharp rise in its net contribution but it is not possible to make an accurate forecast so far ahead. If Britain were faced with too heavy a burden in the 1980s, it is agreed by the Six that 'the very survival of the Community would demand that the institutions find equitable solutions'.

PART SIX—General and Final Provisions

ARTICLES 210 to 240 (summary)

The Community is given legal personality and, under Article 212, the right to lay down the service regulations of its officials. Its headquarters (now provisionally in Brussels) will be finally fixed by 'common accord between member governments' (Article 216).

The rules governing the languages used in the institutions are made unanimously by the Council.

Note: It was agreed that English, Danish and Norwegian would be official languages together with French, German, Italian and Dutch. The Treaties will also be translated into Gaelic for Ireland.

Members agree not to submit a dispute on interpreting the Treaty to any method of settlement other than those provided for. Each member state shall accord the same protection and rights under the same conditions to the nationals of other members as those accorded to its own nationals. Steps will be taken to abolish double taxation in the Common Market. Provisions should, says Article 220, be made for the mutual recognition of firms or companies, for the maintenance of their legal personality in the event of transfer from one member country to another and for the possibility of mergers between firms or companies which are subject to different domestic laws. Formalities for enforcing judgments and arbitration awards are to be 'simplified'.

It is agreed that member states should consult one another to avoid any ill-effects on the Common Market of steps taken by a member in case of serious internal disturbances. Such disturbances are defined as those 'affecting public policy or the maintenance of law and order, in case of war or serious international tension constituting a threat of war, or in order to carry out undertakings a state has entered into for the purpose of maintaining peace and international security' (Article 224). If a state makes improper use of those powers, the Commission or any of the other member states can bring the matter before the European Court which will decide in camera.

The Commission, under Article 228, is responsible for negotiating trade agreements with non-member countries (such as those reached by the Six with Yugoslavia, Israel, Iran, Lebanon and Spain). Article 229 authorises the Commission 'to ensure the maintenance of all appropriate relations with the organs of the United Nations'.

Article 235 provides that the Commission, after consulting the Assembly, should take appropriate steps through the Council when action by the Community is needed to safeguard the Market and the Treaty has not provided the necessary powers. (This was invoked to meet some of the problems which arose over the common agricultural policy due to devaluation of the French franc.)

A conference of member states can be called to amend this Treaty (Article 236).

Any European state may apply to join the Common Market under Article 237 and a unanimous vote of the Council is required for approval of the application. Britain applied under this Article.

Article 238 provides for admission of countries outside the Market to associate membership. *Greece* and *Turkey* became associate members of the Market under this Article.

Protocols annexed to the Treaty are an integral part of it (Article 239).
The Treaty is concluded 'for an unlimited period ' (Article 240).

ARTICLES 241 to 246 (summary)

These cover procedures for the setting up of the Community's institutions.

ARTICLES 247 to 248 (summary)

These provide that the instruments of ratification and authentic texts of the Treaty in French, German, Italian and Dutch are deposited with the Italian Government.

SIGNED AT ROME, MARCH 25TH, 1957, BY:

Belgium: Foreign Minister Paul-Henri Spaak and Baron Jean-Charles Snoy, chief negotiator.

West Germany: Chancellor Konrad Adenauer and Walter Hallstein, Foreign Office State Secretary.

France: Foreign Minister Christian Pineau and Maurice Faure, Foreign Affairs Under Secretary.

Italy: Premier Antonio Segni and Foreign Minister Gaetano Martino.
Luxembourg: Premier Joseph Bech and Lambert Schaus, chief negotiator.
Netherlands: Foreign Minister Joseph Luns and Linthorst Homan, chief negotiator.

Treaty of Accession, Brussels,
22nd January, 1972
PREAMBLE (Summary)

TREATY BETWEEN THE MEMBER STATES OF THE EUROPEAN COMMUNITIES AND THE KINGDOM OF DENMARK, IRELAND, THE KINGDOM OF NORWAY AND THE UNITED KINGDOM OF GREAT BRITAIN AND NORTHERN IRELAND, CONCERNING THE ACCESSION OF THESE FOUR COUNTRIES TO THE COMMON MARKET.

HIS MAJESTY THE KING OF THE BELGIANS, HER MAJESTY THE QUEEN OF DENMARK, THE PRESIDENT OF THE FEDERAL REPUBLIC OF GERMANY, THE PRESIDENT OF THE FRENCH REPUBLIC, THE PRESIDENT OF IRELAND, THE PRESIDENT OF THE ITALIAN REPUBLIC, HIS ROYAL HIGHNESS THE GRAND DUKE OF LUXEMBOURG, HER MAJESTY THE QUEEN OF THE NETHERLANDS, HIS MAJESTY THE KING OF NORWAY, HER MAJESTY THE QUEEN OF THE UNITED KINGDOM OF GREAT BRITAIN AND NORTHERN IRELAND

UNITED in their desire to pursue the attainment of objectives of the Treaty establishing the European Economic Community,

DETERMINED in the spirit of those Treaties to construct an ever closer union among the peoples of Europe on the foundations already laid,

CONSIDERING that Article 237 of the Treaty establishing the European Economic Community . . . affords European states the opportunity of becoming members . . .,

CONSIDERING that the Kingdom of Denmark, Ireland, the Kingdom of Norway and the United Kingdom of Great Britain and Northern Ireland have applied to become members of these Communities,

CONSIDERING that the Council of the European Communities, after having obtained the opinion of the Commission, has declared itself in favour of the admission of these states,

HAVE DECIDED to establish by common agreement the conditions of admission and the adjustments to be made to the Treaty establishing the European Economic Community . . . and to this end have designated as their plenipotentiaries: Here, among the signatures are Edward Heath, Prime Minister, Sir Alec Douglas-Home, Foreign and Commonwealth Secretary, and Geoffrey Rippon, Chief Negotiator.

The above document covers British entry into the Common Market and Euratom. A separate document covers the 'decision of the European Communities Council' to admit the four candidate countries to the Coal and Steel Community. This was because its rules for admitting new members differ from those of the other two Communities.

A third document, the 'act concerning the conditions of accession and the adjustments to the Treaties', incorporates the main body of agreements annexed to the other two documents. The act totals 161 articles which give the force of law to the entry terms and discusses in greater detail the agricultural and financial provisions.

3

THE CHALLENGE TO BRITISH INDUSTRY

No-one expects a sudden change to come over British industry and revitalise it overnight as a result of Britain's entry into the Common Market on January 1, 1973. The full benefits of membership are not likely to be felt for three or four years, which may well be a period of painful readjustment for industry as a whole.

But there is little doubt that such revitalisation will come, bringing with it a surge of expansion, with higher productivity, higher sales, higher investment, higher profits and higher earnings. Despite the argument of anti-Marketeers that circumstances affecting Market members in the past may not necessarily influence Britain in the future, the prevailing, informed view is that Britain has every prospect of experiencing the same economic success as all members of the Six. This will be the result of creating a 'home market' of about 300-million people by removing tariff barriers, compared with the present 'home market' of about 90-million (if European Free Trade Association countries are included). An even more dynamic factor is likely to be the growing trend to 'thinking in Continental terms' when planning production runs, investment and sales, all of which are expected to change radically as Common Market benefits are appreciated.

The effect of having a market of 190-million customers has already been demonstrated by the Six. In the first ten years after formation of the Market, its industrial production rose by four-fifths. In Britain the rise was less than half as much. In the same decade, the gross national product of the Six increased at an annual average rate of 5·1 per cent. In Britain the rate of increase was only 3·2 per cent. All the Six enjoyed growth of GNP, or of private consumption, twice that of Britain.

Other indicators substantiate these results. As Britain's rate of growth in manufacturing capacity fell in recent years, that of the Six showed a further marked increase. During the decade, the Six invested on average 24 per cent of their GNP, while Britain invested only 17 per cent. Trade among the Six, mainly in manufactured goods, increased between 1958 and 1970 by 530 per cent. Britain's total exports doubled between 1958 and 1969; Community's exports, to non-members only, rose by two and a half times.

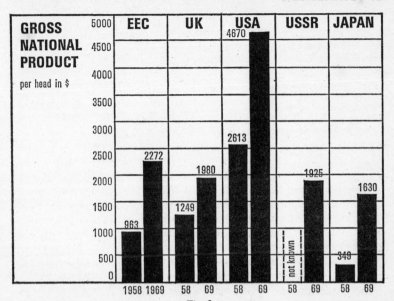

Fig. 2

The GNP for the EEC and its major competititors between 1958 and 1969
(*Source:* EEC Commission).

There seems no reason why Britain should not enjoy equal benefits. The proviso, of course, is that British industry and British firms are ready and able both to take the opportunities offered and meet increased competition in many industries at home from Continental manufacturers. For the enterprising, it will be an exhilarating and rewarding struggle: for the unenterprising, it could mean bankruptcy. But on the whole, British industry believes it can meet the challenge, as a Confederation of British Industry census has indicated. With a few well-known exceptions, such as inshore fishing, hill-farming, horticulture and footwear, industries in all regions are optimistic about their prospects of expansion, even if some expect short-term difficulties and a need for greater investment. As John Davies, Secretary for Trade and Industry, has stated: 'I am in no doubt whatever of these benefits. I am equally in no doubt that practical and intense effort will be needed to enable industry to enjoy them.' Where should this effort be directed?

Preparations
It is essential that if a firm not already established in the Common Market is to make the most of British entry next January, active

preparations should start now. In the view of top industrialists with experience of the Community, British businessmen should already be reviewing their range of products and conducting market research in countries which promise larger sales to establish whether they need modification. Good specialised products offer considerable prospects of success, if competitive on price and capable of maintaining good delivery dates. But different countries have different tastes, even in minor matters such as colours for a well-known brand of sugar-coated chocolate drops which had to be subtly changed for different countries of the Six to ensure a successful sales launching. Other fields of pre-entry consideration are investment in distribution, marketing, transport and depots, branches and sales staff.

Some firms will need local agents. Here, the commercial section of the relevant British Embassy can offer good advice. Embassy commercial sections, as well as the Department of Trade, can also provide expert information on market opportunities and where to place products.

Other companies will prefer to set up foreign subsidiaries and hire local staff. Here, it is important to obtain proper briefing on local pay and conditions, which vary from country to country. Highly important is the need for executives and representatives to gain a working knowledge of the local language where they will operate. Equally vital is to have sales literature ably translated into the appropriate language; it cannot be too strongly recommended to have the text checked by a native of the country involved to avoid howlers. Sales literature should not be left to staff members or others claiming a good knowledge of the foreign language, for errors often happen when this is done.

Bigger companies should consider having their own office or representative in Brussels. Common Market experts emphasise that many regulations are made and negotiations take place all the time which could be of vital interest to British industry, if known about in time. Failing this, companies should consider joining trade associations with offices in Brussels. Some firms might prefer to form an association or merger with a fellow Continental firm. Dunlop and Pirelli have already done this, while other large corporations, such as Beecham's, have taken over Market firms in order to obtain an outlet for their products.

Ideally, firms planning to make the most of the huge new market should have begun their staff work by now, with a view as well to examining how costs can be reduced still further to keep prices as competitive as possible. Probably the most important piece of preparation, however, is a fundamental change of attitude involving a regard for the whole of Western Europe as one sales area, over which representatives can range, and not as a conglomeration of different foreign countries to be approached separately, if at all. As Geoffrey Rippon, Britain's chief negotiator for entry in 1971, has said, there must be an end to 'Market myopia', the tendency to see no further than the Channel.

Tariff Reductions
All industrial tariffs between the United Kingdom and the Six will be eliminated in five equal stages, starting three months after entry. Subject to some special arrangements, Britain will have to apply the Community's Common External Tariff to all countries outside the Community which do not enjoy a privileged relationship with it (see Chapter 2, pp. 36–9.

PROSPECTS FOR INDIVIDUAL INDUSTRIES

In the view of the government, reduction of industrial tariffs between Britain and the other member states of the Common Market will bring 'substantial advantages' and considerable opportunities for British industry. Within three years, British exports will have 'virtually duty-free access' to the large, rapidly-growing market of the Six. Further, in several sectors important to British industry, tariff barriers are still substantial on exports to Europe. They amount to 22 per cent on commercial vehicles, up to 18 per cent on organic chemicals, 16–18 per cent on plastics, 18 per cent on tractors and 14 per cent on diesel engines. Clearly, removal of these tariffs should provide a sharp stimulus.

While entering into the Market should generally act as a spur to the economy, nothing is more difficult than predicting how individual industries and firms will fare. Neither the government nor the Confederation of British Industry have been prepared to commit themselves firmly. Everything depends on the degree of readiness of the individual industry or firm, its will to fight for a share of the new, larger market and the extent to which it meets whatever new, foreign competition there is. All these are imponderables and, doubtlessly, there will be surprise successes and failures once membership becomes an industrial reality. However, there is general optimism through most of industry and through all regions, as a CBI survey confirmed. Whether this optimism is unfounded remains to be seen. Some academic studies on the likely effects have been made. Their base for calculation varies, e.g., one estimates likely comparative effects of tariff reductions on both sides, while another makes predictions after assessments of individual industries. The following indications are based on these studies and on the expectations of various trade associations and companies.

Aerospace

Prospects of expansion are good, particularly through co-operation with EEC firms in such joint projects as the European Airbus, Concorde, the Jaguar fighter and space projects. Further such rationalisation could substantially reduce the extra costs of joint ventures and improve capital efficiency by 10–15 per cent. The British aircraft industry should also benefit from greater readiness of Market countries to invest in joint projects.

Chemicals

Quick benefits are not expected, but the industry is firmly committed to British membership because of anticipated long-term gains from Europe, the only major market still open to trade. An important factor is likely to be the rapid launching of new products.

Exports of organic chemicals and some base chemicals and dyestuffs should rise with the removal of the present high tariff barrier. But inorganic chemicals, pharmaceuticals, synthetic fibres and fertilisers are not expected to benefit greatly and may face stronger Continental competition.

Commodity plastics, such as polyvinyl chloride (PVC), polystyrene and polythene, which form 70 per cent of British output, face keener competition, but benefits may come from rationalisation of investment and greater efficiency. In high value plastics, accounting for 30 per cent of British output, important decisions to relocate about £120-million of new investment in Britain are due following entry. Turnover is expected to rise from the present £100-million to £220-million by 1980 and £360-million by 1985. Benefits are likely to be greatest for the few giant companies and for successful medium and small specialist firms. Altogether, Britain's membership is likely to generate a rise in chemical output of between five and ten per cent.

Coal

At present, the National Coal Board exports $2\frac{1}{2}$-million tons a year to the Economic Community, which imports 30-million tons annually. Prospects of increasing this are regarded as excellent, and British exports to the Market could soon reach at least 5-million tons annually.

Commercial Vehicles

These are expected to gain more than almost any other in the Common Market with the removal of the 22 per cent tariff. The British industry is easily the strongest in Europe, both in capacity and ability to offer good prices. Sales of medium trucks will make the biggest initial impact, but light and heavy vehicles are expected to follow. Increased sales of European makes, such as Volkswagen and Fiat, are also expected here. Harmonisation of truck regulations should aid British manufacturers to exploit the fast-growing trans-Continental heavy truck market.

Computers

Hopes of more profitable exports through lower tariffs and a possible merger between Britain's ICL and a Continental competitor have diminished. Three leading European companies, Siemens, Philips and the French CII, announced a new grouping in February, 1972. ICL, which has been promised substantial government aid, still hopes to compete successfully with its large customer base, established models and a new series under development. Important gains may also be made by integral circuits and semi-conductors through accelerated growth and rationalisation of British multi-national firms.

Diesel Engines

British manufacturers, already the world's major producers of high-speed diesel engines, are confident of long-term sales prospects and are anxious to make further inroads into the European market. One firm, Cummins, is spending £2-million over three years developing its European sales and service network, and expects to increase production from 25-thousand to 87-thousand engines a year by 1980. Competition is threatened not only from German, but also from Japanese manufacturers.

Electrical Plant

British manufacturers are hopeful of long-term gains, but much depends on developing Continental markets by the removal of national buying barriers to British tenders for power stations and other heavy plants. This is expected to happen between 1975 and the 1980s and is likely to be accompanied by further international mergers and link-ups which could benefit the industry.

General Engineering

Prospects of the industry, which employs more than three-million workers, of benefiting from British membership depend on its recovery from its present depressed condition and a reduction in the rate of wage and cost inflation. Subject to this, there is optimism, and successful specialist firms will undoubtedly thrive.

Among the most recent evidence of how the industry views its prospects is a survey by *The Engineer* of 254 British companies. It showed that three-quarters of the firms in manufacturing engineering expect to benefit from Market entry. Only three per cent expected to be worse off. More than 70 per cent expected to increase their sales volume by between six and 20 per cent, although half believed the rise would be between six and ten per cent. Nearly half the British companies did not expect to change their products.

The survey also disclosed that British engineering management was weaker in corporate planning for entry than American management, which seemed already geared to anticipate British entry. As many as 30 per cent were unlikely to accelerate plans as a result of the decision to enter the Market, but 60 per cent thought they would probably do so. About half the small British companies seemed less optimistic. Firms seeing the greatest benefits were those with more than £5-million turnover.

Growth areas were seen by 79 per cent of firms to be in the United Kingdom, while 68 per cent saw it taking place on the Continent. Costs were expected to rise by 37 per cent of companies, with highest increases for the small firm, and only 36 per cent thought costs would be the same. Few British firms believed they would need extra labour, and 50 per cent foresaw sales and marketing as the functions in greatest demand.

Firms were wary of predicting changes in volumes of specific sales, expected substantially increased competition and the need to readapt gradually, after which full advantages could be achieved. Failure to meet delivery deadlines would jeopardise chances.

Footwear

This is one of the British industries facing a major threat after Market entry, which is expected to bring a flood of quality shoes from Italian and other manufacturers. By 1980, a survey has warned, the industry could suffer an overall 10 per cent drop in production, and up to 20 per cent in vital, everyday shoes. The industry has been warned it must increase quality of design, cut labour costs and increase exporting efforts. Failing that, present imports of 27 per cent of the British market could rise to 50 per cent by 1980. Prospects for higher exports to Europe are poor without wholesale changes in production, design and marketing to overcome previous neglect of European markets.

Furniture

Firms should do well provided they ensure good design, competitive prices and prompt delivery. The Market offers an additional 59-million households. There should be increased opportunities for knock-down furniture, avoiding high freight charges. One firm is already doing well in Germany as a result of attractive design and quality.

Machine Tools

Stiffer competition is expected from strong German firms, which may bring difficulties for some British general tool builders. But successful British specialist firms should achieve greater market penetration. Britain's strong numerical control industry should do well, which may result in British control systems being attached to foreign tools. Membership may also lead to further regroupings and concentration, and greater competitive strength.

Motors

Despite the capture by Market manufacturers of a much larger share of the British market over the past 18 months, British car manufacturers are also confident of making good progress in Europe, even though some short-term disadvantages may be felt. British Leyland has estimated that its sales in Europe outside Britain could rise from 200-thousand to 500-thousand cars by 1975–6. Of these, 270-thousand will be from Continental assembly plants. Investment in Europe will also rise substantially.

The Society of Motor Manufacturers has also estimated that within five years of entry, the net balance of payments in vehicles and components is likely to be £200- to £300-million better than if Britain remained outside. But substantial investment is regarded as necessary to meet increased competition.

Nevertheless, as Continental distributors have made clear, success by British cars in the Market is by no means automatic. Models must be attractive, well-finished, competitive in price and delivery, and there is an urgent need to develop service facilities, particularly in Germany. A decrease in highly-damaging strikes in the motor industry would obviously boost British exports efforts and the industry's reputation. A further result of entry may be that more American investment, which has been increasing in the Community, will return to Britain.

Nuclear Energy
Best prospects of increased sales seem likely through greater co-operation with European consortia on joint projects. Already, considerable formal co-operation exists.

Pottery
Accession to the larger market is expected to provide extra business and improve the present depressed state of the British industry.

Steel
The British Steel Corporation expects to make important gains from British membership. These will largely be in increased deliveries to British consumers benefitting from entry and increased sales, but it also expects to increase direct exports to Europe. There may well be increased specialisation, with abandonment of production of some items which Continental manufacturers can produce cheaper, with increased concentration on items in which Britain has recognised skills, such as rolling sheet steel for cars, refrigerators and other consumer durables.

Textiles
Prospects are mixed. Woollen goods, carpets, linen fabrics, weft knitting and some other items are expected to do well, but artificial fibres, knitwear, cotton fabrics and clothing accessories will face sharp competition. Higher exports of made-up clothing may depend on penetration by British firms of the Continental retail market, such as Burton's success in France.

European Coal and Steel Community
Britain, as well as entering the Common Market and Euratom (atomic energy), will also join the European Coal and Steel Community (ECSC), created in 1952. This will result in removal of price, duty and other barriers to trade between Britain and the other Market countries and acceptance of a common set of rules and development policies. Pooling of the coal, steel and iron industries of the Six in this way resulted in a considerable increase in business between them. In 1970, the Community produced 109·2-million metric tons of steel against 125·2-million in the United States, 110·2-million in the Soviet Union (in 1969) and 26·3-million in Britain.

To co-ordinate coal and steel production, the Community has direct powers to fix price lists, authorise investment programmes and research grants, impose fines on firms for breaches of rules and collect a tax on production. It also imposes strict anti-trust laws to ensure free competition. The Community has also furthered mergers of steel-producing units with the aim of creating about ten large efficient firms capable of competing efficiently in world markets. Already, there are several companies with an annual output of five-million tons or more, though none so large as the British Steel Corporation. It has spent about £400-million further investment on coal and steel modernisation projects.

Fears have been expressed by observers that control of the British coal and steel industries, each of which will be the largest single unit in the Community, will be handed over to Eurocrats. But during the negotiations, the Six made it clear that they did not intend to question the size or system of ownership of either the National Coal Board or the British Steel Corporation, and that these industries' relationship with the British government would not only continue almost unchanged, but would probably have greater autonomy than hitherto, since the European Coal and Steel Treaty stipulates complete managerial independence and responsibility. Some changes in present legislation will be involved, but, to all intents and purposes, both British industries will operate as before except with the advantage of a substantially larger market.

This should be especially beneficial for coal, of which the Community imports about 30-million tons annually. Demand for it has fallen substantially in the Community, as in Britain, the result of growing competition from oil, natural gas and other sources of energy. Altogether, the Community produces about 170-million tons of coal annually (about the same as by Britain), expected to fall to 144-million tons by 1975. Free movement of labour will be restricted with British membership: in the coal and steel industries, it is limited to a few categories of skilled, experienced workers, and there is no danger of an influx of dangerously inexperienced foreign labour into British mines or steelworks.

In addition to supervising coal and steel production and management, the Coal and Steel Community has worked to assist its workers. It has retrained about 400-thousand men and has provided financial assistance for new housing with loans of up to 50 per cent of construction costs. By the end of 1970, the Community had financed construction of 113,011 dwellings at a total cost of about £475-million, of which the Community's contribution in loans was about £110-million.

Workers made redundant are also aided by allowances to help them until they find new jobs. Those forced to take less well-paid jobs have their wages supplemented by grants, and workers moving to new areas receive resettlement payments. More than one-thousand miners' orphans have been aided by post-school educational grants. New industries have been encouraged by loans to come to areas where the coal industry is contracting. So far, 1·5-million workers have benefitted. There has been substantial expenditure on medical and social research and on safety.

When Britain is a full member, these benefits, some of which already exist here, will be extended in full to British coal and steel workers. Also, British iron, coal and steel workers, as well as the National Coal Board and the British Steel Corporation and their consumers, will be represented in strength in the European Consultative Committee of the Coal and Steel Community, and will have an important role in the formation of future policy.

Britain's contribution to the Community's reserve fund, of which the total is £90-million, will be £24-million, to be paid in three stages from January 1, 1973. Almost all of Britain's contribution will be spent on its own industry. Several million pounds will also be paid by the National Coal Board and British Steel Corporation in a levy on turnover to cover administrative expenses and financial grants. Leaders of the nationalised industries, particularly of the Coal Board, have strongly supported British entry.

European Atomic Energy Community (Euratom)
In an attempt to catch up with, or at least to reduce the lead of, the United States, the Soviet Union and Britain in the field of peaceful nuclear development, the Six, simultaneously with the Common Market in 1958, launched a separate Community, the European Atomic Energy Community.

Known as Euratom, this Community's main function is to encourage the member states to pool their research efforts to develop nuclear power. It was also intended that it help in using radio isotopes and radio-active sources for agricultural, industrial and medical purposes, pool and distribute scientific information and train scientists and technicians.

The many disputes between France and its partners on how Euratom should be run have dimmed hopes of the founders that this might be the most important of the Communities. Britain undertook to share in the cost of running it with the other countries in an enlarged Market. British negotiators said that Britain would be prepared to pass on to the Six some of its non-military nuclear 'knowhow' in certain circumstances.

The *Joint Research Centre* of Euratom which was set up between 1959 and 1961 with 2,500 scientists and other staff consists of four establishments: *Ispra*, north of Milan, Italy, concentrates on heavy-water reactors and fundamental research; *Geel*, Belgium, the Central Nuclear Measurements Bureau; *Karlsruhe*, West Germany, the European Transuranium Institute; and *Petten*, the Netherlands, a general purpose establishment.

In December 1969, the Six agreed to reorganise Euratom and give it powers to carry out nuclear research under contract for clients in the Community and extend its activity to non-nuclear scientific research projects. The direction of Euratom should, it was agreed, be 'streamlined' and this and other reforms should become effective in 1972. Studies have begun to decide which process is most suitable for a European uranium enrichment plant.

Energy: the need for a special policy
The movement towards a Common Market energy policy is sluggish owing to conflicting interests and existing disparities. Italy has no coal industry; Germany is engaged in a careful running down of coal; the Netherlands has virtually abandoned coal; France, and more recently West Germany, are preoccupied with developing their own oil industries.

The emphasis is on a mixture of state control of energy, notably in France and Italy, and subsidies, principally to protect coal. Britain, with its nationalised energy industries of coal, gas and electricity and nuclear energy, will merely be adding size to the problems, not changing their nature.

The production of a meaningful energy policy has been a long-standing Market issue. An inter-executive working group was established as long ago as 1958 and six years later there was a broad declaration of intent, that policy should be based on cheapness and security of supply.

Three bodies traditionally share responsibility for energy: the coal wing of ECSC, Euratom (nuclear power) and the EEC Commission (oil and natural gas). The institutional barrier has been partly overcome with the merger, four years ago, of the executive machinery. But variations in the Treaties of Rome, Paris and Euratom still present administrative problems that will be overcome only by a single treaty covering energy.

In more practical terms, the fundamental change in the shape of the energy market during the past decade has produced major problems both on the fuel and social fronts and reinforced the case for a more effective policy. On the one hand, coal's declining importance has been accompanied by the need to erect protectionist barriers and phase the rundown in manpower as well as production without producing massive unemployment and additional social burdens. On the other, the growth in demand for cheaper oil has made the Community increasingly dependent on external sources of energy and more vulnerable to any interruption in supply. Britain's entry coincides with fresh attempts to overhaul the existing policy.

The upheavals created by the changing relationships between the oil companies and the producing countries has ended the era of cheap oil and caused governments to look more closely at energy policies and security of supply. The Six import about 97 per cent of their crude oil needs and oil accounts for almost 60 per cent of energy consumption. Coal is now down to 27 per cent and natural gas nine per cent, although the proportion varies among member countries.

The new objectives on oil involve countries disclosing details of stocks and import volumes, providing notification of investments planned by oil companies creating a Common Market 'stocking' programme and bringing fuel taxes into line. These guidelines should not inhibit competition, says the EEC Commission, and the emphasis should continue to be on market forces rather than intervention and the interests of consumers should continue to take priority over those of producers.

One of the most important policy moves involves increasing oil and product reserves from the present 65 days to about 90 days consumption. This costly programme represents a massive increase in capacity and underground storage is being pressed as one avenue worth exploring.

The objects are to provide a more effective buffer against interruption in supplies, easing the problems of co-ordination when difficulties emerge, and to harmonise the myriad of regulations. There is also a strong feeling that oil companies should be given additional financial and tax advantages to encourage their development, as well as strengthen trading links with the producing countries, thereby improving the political climate.

At present, energy policy does not present major difficulties for Britain's fuel industries. Oil reserves have traditionally been equivalent to three months' supply. Gas, however, could see its 'monopoly' powers as a purchaser of North Sea gas undermined. Coal expects to gain a substantial outlet in a market which still needs to import about 25-million tons a year from non-EEC sources. It needs to change its pricing structure, as does steel, to allow for deduction of the transport element (customers nearer coal mines and steel mills will feel the benefit) and create more room for manoeuvre as a result of less government intervention.

Britain's long and expensive experience with nuclear energy already forms the basis for co-operative projects and there will undoubtedly be room for others within the framework of Euratom.

Regional Policy

A common regional policy, or rather a policy for aiding under-developed regions, is still being formulated in the European Economic Community after years of fruitless negotiations among the Six. The Community Commission hopes that British entry will end the dead-lock, an essential step for further healthy development of the Common Market. Hitherto, individual member states have devel-oped, and are still developing, a wide range of measures aimed at tackling their own regional problems, many of which, such as taxa-tion incentives, preferential loans, building and retraining grants, are very similar to those in Britain. But it has always been recognised that conflicting national policies should first be supplemented, then harmonised.

At present, wealth and expansion in the Community are tending to concentrate more and more in the 'central areas', the industrialised heartlands of the Ruhr, Low Countries, northern and eastern France, southern West Germany and northern Italy, in which 40 per cent of the Community population live. Outlying regions, such as southern Italy, southern and southwest France and the stretch of West Germany along the border with East Germany, are underdeveloped. About 50-million people, or a quarter of the Community's popula-tion, live in thinly-populated agricultural areas. These imbalances within the Community have grown with its dynamic expansion.

Some areas have become depopulated, while other regions, with better roads, transport and other infra-structures, have attracted investment and workers in large numbers. Some farming areas have undergone complete changes. Coastal regions close to deep seaports have flourished, for instance, through the siting of huge new steel plants accessible to large ore-carriers, while other inland industrial areas have declined. There are now fears that not only could the crowded heartlands of the Community face unprecedented pollution, but many fringe areas become derelict.

Once a Community regional policy is agreed upon, British development areas will stand to receive substantial benefits which could largely offset the high cost of British entry. These areas include the Northeast, the Southwest and parts of Scotland, Wales and Northern Ireland. The common regional policy would supplement existing national policies, and the special needs of backward British areas would be taken into account by Brussels planners. The policy will also ensure that international companies cannot play one Market country off against another by exploiting taxation incentives and making large profits in rich industrial regions while doing little to help more depressed areas. A common regional policy will also lay down joint rules on investment to ensure that development areas are given priority by investors. It is also expected to aim at developing all backward areas adequately in the interests of all. The whole of Ireland will be regarded as requiring 'special regional treatment' once the Republic joins.

Some observers have suggested that with the 'centre of gravity' of the Market lying in the Rhine–Ruhr region, outlying and under-developed areas of Britain will inevitably suffer from membership. This is not borne out by Community experience, which shows that regional disparity of unemployment and incomes has been substan-tially reduced in recent years. Although concern is felt about some problem industries, such as inshore fishing, hill farming and horti-culture, this pessimism is not shared by industry in the regions con-cerned, all of which are confident they can compete successfully despite some short-term difficulties. Clearly, communications in all regions must be improved if industry is to take advantage of the larger market.

In general, Market membership is not expected to inhibit the continuation of British regional policy, and Britain, with her long experience of regional planning and policies, is expected to have an important say in development of the joint Community policy. Further, the expected growth of the British economy following Market entry should make possible financing of more successful home development policies. With full British membership, American and other foreign firms are more likely to invest here, following a relative decline of such investment in favour of the Community, and this investment is likely to be attracted by special incentives to development areas.

Meanwhile, the Community has not been idle in giving regional aid despite the absence of a common policy. In addition to very substantial aid for coal and steel industries, the European Investment Bank has loaned more than £600-million for regional developments, more than 1·3-million workers have been retrained with aid from the European Social Fund amounting to another £600-million and grants of £600 agreed for each job created by companies for farmers under 55 and their children who agree to leave the land. Ministers of the Six have also agreed in principle to impose a ceiling of 20 per cent on incentives to investments in 'central areas' and may introduce a Market interest-rebate fund for loans to finance special projects in selected regions.

PROSPECTS FOR WORKERS AND UNIONS

Almost all British unions, with a few notable exceptions, have come out against Common Market entry, as did the Trades Union Congress. The TUC's attitude, partly influenced by the pre-determined standpoints of its large left-wing unions, is based on the short-term effects of entry on the cost of living and on a projection of the effect of the balance of payments by 1980. Other unions have taken similar lines, in part to maintain links with the Labour Party. It is perhaps noteworthy that some of the more important unions, whose leaders favour entry, include the General and Municipal Workers, the Electricians and the Clerical Workers.

It is likely that once Market membership becomes a part of industrial life in Britain, the unions will respond by quickly exploiting the opportunities offered to raise wages and conditions to Continental standards, and to the prospect of developing international bargaining and co-operation with Common Market unions. A fundamental transformation of union thinking is likely to be achieved in bargaining concepts, and unions will become active protagonists of the European idea, whatever their political views.

For union members and workers, Market entry will assume little importance at first, although higher living costs may stimulate wages demands. The prospective benefits in higher wages and better conditions to be gained from international bargaining and more rapidly rising productivity should activate union officials. Greater competition, already to be seen in the motor industry where Continental car manufacturers have increased their share of the British market to more than 20 per cent in the last year or so, may well indirectly lead to a reduced number of strikes. Once the Market has become an everyday reality, there is room for optimism that the majority of British industrial workers will be 'thinking European' within a few years. Summer holidays and car ownership have already created a greater awareness in the working force of the proximity of Europe.

4

THE COMMON LABOUR MARKET

As of January 1, 1973, a British worker will be able to get a job anywhere in the nine other member countries without a special labour permit or visa. He can go to any of them to look for work, or to take a prearranged job as freely as, say, a worker in England can look for or take a job in Scotland. Once he takes the job in any of the other member countries, he can settle there with the same rights as those of the citizens of that country. Workers in the nine other member states are equally free to look for and to take jobs in Britain.

This free movement of workers is provided for in Articles 48 to 51 of the Rome Treaty, under which the Six established a common labour market (see Chapter 2). The free movement rules do not apply to the civil service, in which each member state is entitled to give priority to its own nationals.

Some observers have expressed fears that the relaxation of traditional British immigration barriers against other Market workers, as provided for in Market rules, will lead to an influx of foreign labour. But the opposite is likely to be true. Few Common Market workers can be expected to be attracted by the lower wages, poorer social benefits, fewer holidays and substantially higher unemployment now pertaining to this country.

All these factors may influence more British workers to go to work in Europe. In West Germany, where demand for labour is highest and prospects best, the number of Britons rose from 13-thousand at the beginning of 1971 to 17-thousand in August, and was expected to reach 20-thousand by early 1972. Some experts have predicted that between 150-thousand and 200-thousand Britons could be working in Germany by 1980, if current trends continue.

Towards the end of the British entry negotiations, the Six were considering whether special rules might be needed for British Commonwealth immigrants seeking work in other Market member countries.

Wages

In 1958, when the Common Market was formed, British workers were better off than those of any Market country. Now they have been overtaken by workers in every Market country, with the possible exception of Italy, where lower pay is made up by substantial fringe benefits. It has been estimated that if Britain had entered the Community in 1958 and enjoyed the same growth, the average male worker would be at least £7 a week better off than now.

In the Common Market generally, average earnings have risen faster and are higher for comparable employment than in Britain. Fringe benefits paid for by employers, such as holidays, Christmas bonuses and social security payments, are also substantially better. This higher prosperity has been made possible by much greater increases in productivity. Income tax and tax on expenditure in most Market countries are also lower than in Britain, particularly for the low-paid.

An indication of how incomes have risen faster in the Community than in Britain is provided by the following table. It shows average incomes per employed person in dollars, including social security contributions and fringe benefits paid by employers, but excluding self-employed and unearned income:

	1958	1969	% Change
Belgium	1,846	3,811	+106
France	1,730	4,176	+170
Germany	1,461	3,470	+123
Italy	1,033	2,812	+172
Luxembourg*	2,488	4,037	+ 62
Netherlands	1,432	3,987	+165
Community	1,455	3,566	+145
United Kingdom	1,677	2,779	+ 93

*The Luxembourg figures refer to 1960–1968.

Source: ECSO.

The higher fringe benefits in the Community are shown by the following table, giving a breakdown for 1968:

	Cost as % add to wage costs	Social Sec.	Family Allow.	Hols.	Bonus, Bounties	Other benefits
Belgium	54·4	16·2	10·5	17·4	5·1	5·2
France	70·0	18·3	13·3	13·3	8·2	16·9
Germany	44·5	15·9	—	14·5	4·3	9·8
Italy	91·9	28·8	17·4	18·2	17·3	10·2
Luxembourg	40·8	14·6	4·0	10·5	6·1	5·6
Netherlands	49·9	12·0	5·5	10·6	8·2	13·6
United Kingdom	22·2	5·9	—	7·8	2·4	6·1

Source: EEC.

Although prices have also risen in the Community, and for food are often higher than in Britain, real wages have gone up two to three times as fast as here after allowing for higher living costs. This is illustrated by the following table showing trends in wages and living costs within each country, but not comparative living costs and wage levels between countries (1958 = 100):

	Retail Price Index 1970	Gross hourly wages index 1970	Real Wages Rise %
Belgium	137	214	56
France	164	252	54
Germany	133	259	95
Italy	148	284	92
Luxembourg	130	215	62
Netherlands	159	275	73
United Kingdom	151	196	30

It is difficult to make true comparisons of actual earnings. However, the accompanying table gives gross and net earnings for five varied occupations. It should be borne in mind that while deductions are often substantial in the Community, benefits, notably retirement pensions, are much better than in Britain. Hours worked in the Community are marginally less, and holidays considerably greater.

When British membership in the Market begins to make its impact on industry, there will undoubtedly be pressure from unions to bring pay, holidays and other benefits into line with European levels. Economic pressures will also inevitably militate for such improvements, and the higher productivity which membership is expected to bring should also result in higher real wages.

Social Security
None of the Common Market countries has a comprehensive social security system and National Health Service such as Britain's; the NHS will be unaffected by entry. But all members of the Six spend more on social welfare than we do. In 1968, the latest available year, total expenditure per head of the population was: Belgium £148, France £149, Germany £169, Italy £98, Luxembourg £98, Netherlands £145 and Britain £95.

Much of the higher Community expenditure is accounted for by higher pensions, family allowances and other benefits. The higher benefits account for the high deductions from salaries, since welfare is based on contributions rather than taxation as in Britain. In recent years, all Community members have initiated streamlining and harmonisation of social security provisions, and have studied Britain's Health Service as a model.

EARNINGS AND WORKING HOURS OF FIVE OCCUPATIONS IN THE
COMMUNITY AND BRITAIN, JULY, 1970, EXPRESSED IN AMERICAN DOLLARS

PRIMARY SCHOOL TEACHER, AGED 30, MARRIED, NO CHILDREN

City	Gross Annual Earnings $	Spendable after Tax $	Spendable after Tax % of Gross Earnings	Spendable after Tax & Soc. Sec. Contributions $	% of Gross	Working Week Hours
Amsterdam	4,194	3,569	85·1	3,370	80·4	25*
Brussels	3,366	2,981	88·5	2,686	79·8	26
Düsseldorf	5,945	4,979	83·8	4,277	71·9	30
Luxembourg	4,836	4,222	87·3	3,951	81·7	29
Milan	2,910	2,636	90·6	2,571	88·4	30
Paris	2,718	2,540	93·5	2,362	86·9	30
London	2,877	2,397	83·3	2,133	74·2	35

*Lessons.

BUS DRIVER, 10 YEARS EXPERIENCE, 35, MARRIED, TWO CHILDREN

City						
Amsterdam	4,810	4,267	88·7	3,993	83·0	42½
Brussels	3,192	2,958	92·7	2,607	81·7	43
Düsseldorf	4,167	3,756	90·2	3,217	77·2	43
Luxembourg	4,565	4,335	95·0	4,098	89·8	40
Milan	4,372	3,884	88·8	3,620	82·8	39½
Paris	3,261	3,096	94·9	2,879	88·3	42½
London	3,116	2,708	86·9	2,433	78·1	50

SKILLED AUTOMOBILE MECHANIC, ABOUT 5 YEARS EXPERIENCE, 25, SINGLE

City						
Amsterdam	3,934	3,421	87·0	2,520	64·0	42½
Brussels	3,065	2,802	91·4	2,528	82·5	43
Düsseldorf	3,798	3,166	83·4	2,667	70·2	40
Luxembourg	3,614	3,187	88·2	2,790	77·2	48
Milan	2,433	2,309	94·9	2,133	87·7	42
Paris	2,899	2,607	89·9	2,426	83·7	50
London	2,637	2,157	81·8	1,906	72·3	45

BANK TELLER, TRAINED, 10 YEARS EXPERIENCE, MARRIED, TWO CHILDREN

City						
Amsterdam	6,307	5,522	87·6	4,522	71·7	40
Brussels	5,122	4,693	91·6	4,369	85·3	40
Düsseldorf	5,725	4,990	87·2	4,307	75·2	41¼
Luxembourg	4,899	4,520	92·3	4,052	82·7	40
Milan	6,589	5,730	87·0	5,301	80·5	38¾
Paris	3,623	3,551	98·0	3,188	88·0	40
London	3,596	3,140	87·3	2,841	79·0	41

SECRETARY OF DEPARTMENT HEAD, 3 YEARS EXPERIENCE, SHORTHAND-TYPING,
ONE FOREIGN LANGUAGE, 22, SINGLE

City						
Amsterdam	2,869	2,538	88·5	2,152	75·0	40
Brussels	3,173	2,864	90·3	2,594	81·7	44
Düsseldorf	4,073	3,363	82·6	2,832	69·5	40
Luxembourg	3,357	2,961	88·2	2,660	79·2	40
Milan	3,124	2,825	90·4	2,594	83·0	42
Paris	4,167	3,768	90·4	3,352	80·4	40
London	2,877	2,302	80·0	2,038	70·8	40

Source: Union Bank of Switzerland: Prices and Earnings Around the Globe.

Sickness Insurance

It is compulsory for employees in Common Market countries to insure themselves against medical treatment by paying contributions to a sick provident fund or medical insurance company. In some, it is voluntary above a certain income level, but almost everyone is insured in one way or another.

In Germany, the Netherlands and Italy, and in France for miners, the doctor, chemist or hospital is paid directly by the sickness insurance fund, although the employee may have to contribute to the cost of treatment. In the other three member countries, the patient pays the medical fees, but usually regains 75–80 per cent of the total cost from the fund. Hospital treatment is usually free for lower-paid workers. As in Britain, most Market countries have minor prescription charges.

In general, sick insurance is more expensive than in Britain, and it costs more to be ill, and appreciably more for dental treatment. For a major operation or treatment, the Common Market system cannot compare with the National Health Service.

Finally, Community wage-earners and their families on holiday in other member countries can receive medical treatment on the same terms as local citizens, and this will be available to Britons after entry.

Pensions

Pensions, both state old-age and other retirement pensions, tend to be substantially higher in Community countries than in Britain. Only the Netherlands has a national pensions scheme with a flat-rate pension similar to that of Britain, but, there, a married couple receives nearly £16 a week, with a holiday bonus of £48 a year, compared to £9·70 in Britain.

All other Market countries have pensions graded according to contributions paid in, which depend again on the previous wage or salary of the insured person. Rates of contribution and benefit also vary, and statutory schemes may be supplemented by extra pensions achieved through collective bargaining. But in all the Six, pensions are linked to the cost of living, as in Italy and Belgium, or to the general level of earnings as in West Germany, where they are raised annually.

The result is that in Belgium, people receive about 75 per cent of average earnings for all years of covered employment, in Germany 60–65 per cent of last annual earnings, in France about 35 per cent of average earnings over the final ten years' employment, in Italy 74 per cent of average earnings of the final, best-paid three years after 40 years covered employment, and in Luxembourg 60–80 per cent of final annual earnings.

Although the government has promised to help pensioners meet higher food prices when we enter, Britain is also expected to come under increasing pressure to improve her pensions and review them more often to match Market standards. Considerable improvements would eventually come about under plans for supplementary pensions, but these would be long-term from 1975 if the scheme were introduced.

Family Allowances
These vary widely among the Six, but in almost every respect are higher, sometimes substantially, than in Britain. All but West Germany pay an allowance for the first child. For families with three children, monthly allowances in July, 1970, amounted to: Germany £8·58, Italy £11 and Belgium more than £26, with others ranging within these. In Britain, the corresponding figure was £8·21. British workers taking permanent jobs in Market countries will be entitled to allowances.

Holidays
Annual holidays in the Community are much longer and public holidays more numerous than in Britain. Workers in Belgium are entitled to 18 days, France 24 days, West Germany 15–24 days, Luxembourg 18–24 days, the Netherlands 10–24 days, and Italy 12–30 days annual paid holiday. In Britain workers are entitled to 10–15 days holiday a year.

Public holidays amount to: Belgium 10, France 8–10, Germany 10–13, Italy 17, Luxembourg 10, the Netherlands seven days. In Britain, there are only six public or bank holidays.

Market membership is expected to make British standards correspond more with those of the Six.

Industrial Relations
In general, collective bargaining and conclusion of agreements in the Common Market are subject to legislation; an agreement is ordinarily legally binding once signed by both sides. There is a greater recourse to industrial courts to settle disputes than has been the case in Britain prior to the Industrial Relations Act. In some countries, the state also plays an active role by extending negotiated agreements to apply throughout an industry, particularly one in which workers are not organised.

The incidence of strikes varies widely between members of the Six, but unofficial, or wildcat, strikes which have been prevalent in Britain are comparatively rare because of the legal consequences. On the other hand, some Market members, notably Italy and France, have been badly hit by stoppages, although those in Italy, in particular, tend to be short token stoppages because of union weakness.

Some indication of the proneness to strikes of Market members is given in the following table of days lost through disputes per 1,000 workers in mining, manufacturing, transport and construction:

	1969	Annual Average 1965–69
Belgium	100	156
France	200	243*
Germany	20	10
Italy	4,110	1,574
Netherlands	10	12
United Kingdom	510	294

*1968 omitted from French average because of abnormal June losses.

Source: DE and ILO.

In Britain, there has been a sharp decline in the number of strikes, if not in the number of working days lost, during the past year. If this trend continues, reinforced by the operation of the Industrial Relations Act, Britain may well compare more favourably in future.

Another aspect of industrial relations which is more highly developed in the Community than in Britain is workers' participation in management. This is especially advanced in Germany, where there are plans to extend it still further. Works councils are founded on law, and in Germany there are workers' representatives on supervisory and management boards, i.e. worker-directors.

Under the Community Commission's plans for a 'European company' statute, which would enable firms to operate fully throughout the Market, works councils and workers' directors are proposed even if there is no provision for them under individual member states' law. Eventually, such innovations should come in British industry also.

Unions

Trade union organisation inside the Community, though strong in membership in some countries, is fragmented. Only West Germany, whose Deutscher Gewerkschaftsbund has 6·7-million members, has a central federation which compares with Britain's Trades Union Congress, with ten-million affiliated members. In other countries, such as Italy, union claims are often considerably higher than realistic assessments of actual membership.

In these countries, unions form separate groupings according to politics and religion, mainly Social Democrat, Christian and Communist. In Germany, Belgium and the Netherlands, unions are powerful organisations, while they are weak in France and Italy, where Communist groups predominate. In the whole Community, there are only 17-million trade unionists, of which 11-million belong to unions affiliated to the International Confederation of Free Trade Unions. Communist unions are excluded from this, and are affiliated to the Communist World Federation of Trade Unions.

In recent years, co-ordination of union activity inside the Community has developed, and in 1969, the ICFTU unions formed a 'Market TUC', the European Confederation of Free Trade Unions, with which the British TUC has maintained close links. Both the ICFTU and Christian unions fully support European integration, and as the Community has progressed and brought prosperity to workers, even the Communist unions of France and Italy have come round to give it qualified support. As a result, both the French CGT and Italian CGIL Communist groups now sit with other unions on the Community's Economic and Social Committee.

In general, unions would like a more important role in the formation and execution of Market policies. There is no doubt that once Britain is a full member, the TUC, which has held a watching brief in Brussels for many years, will play a major role in top-level consultations and possibly assume the leadership of European unions.

With development of a larger Community, there is also likely to be an extension of inter-union co-operation and of international bargaining with multi-national corporations. British workers taking jobs in Europe will enjoy the legal right to belong to a union or, in Germany and France, not to join one. They will also be entitled to reciprocal union benefits if they are union members in Britain.

5

THE COMMON AGRICULTURAL MARKET

The common agricultural policy of the Six means that, ultimately, all foodstuffs produced by farms in all member states will flow freely between all Market members. The tariff, levy and quota barriers between Britain and the rest of the Common Market must, subject to certain safeguard arrangements to deal with such changes as in the value of currencies, be abolished. Under the British entry terms this is to be done gradually within five years, from the date of accession, January 1, 1973.

By 1978, therefore, Britain, as the terms stand, becomes part of a common market for farm goods similar to, but in some ways much more closely integrated, than the common market for manufactured goods described in Chapter 4.

The common agricultural policy, generally referred to as the CAP, not only allows free flow of farm goods but provides that many should be sold on the basis of a common prices structure. It applies to and creates common organisations of the market for the following products: *cereals, butter, cheese, milk, beef, veal, pork, bacon, sugar, olive* and other *oils, oilseeds, poultry, eggs, hops, tobacco, rice, wine, fruit, vegetables, fish, flax, hemp.*

When British entry negotiations on the terms were completed in 1971, CAP did not cover mutton, lamb and potatoes.

The common prices structure means that the price of a loaf of bread or a joint of meat in Britain and the greater part of Western Europe will be decided to a great extent by ministers of the member states in the Brussels Council. CAP therefore has a direct impact on the cost of living.

To maintain farm prices at similar levels in all member states (with special exceptions), there are common systems of market support varying as to product. To protect member states' farmers and food traders, a common barrier, in the form of levies on agricultural imports from external markets, will be placed around Britain and its partners in the common farm market by 1977. Some products, e.g. vegetables, are protected by CET.

Finally, the members have agreed to assume joint responsibility for meeting the cost of the agricultural market support system and, to a limited but increasing extent, for the cost of modernising and generally improving the efficiency of their national agricultures. The bills are paid through a common budget almost the whole of which is now devoted to farm expenditure.

The budget system and Ministerial Council and Commission thus function in some ways as a Western European Ministry of Agriculture. This is the furthest the national governments of the Six have gone in allowing Brussels institutions to exercise federal-type powers. If they wish, however, the member national governments can, by unanimous vote in the Ministerial Council, change the common rules or, indeed, change the entire policy.

Precedents for suspending the full application of the policy have already been established. For instance, as a result of the devaluation of the franc and the revaluation of the Deutsche Mark, trade barriers in farm goods between some member states had to be temporarily restored. This was because the CAP expresses the common prices in *units of account* which are linked to gold and, until the currency realignments of late 1971, were equal in value to the U.S. dollar. Thus, when West Germany floated the deutschemark upwards its farmers, under the CAP rules, began receiving fewer units of account for their goods. A similar situation arose in the Netherlands when the guilder was changed in value. A system of levies and rebates therefore had to be applied at frontiers between Market countries to prevent trade distortion.

Although such emergency measures can be taken, the basic framework which binds the national agricultures together is expected to be a permanent one. The 1971 setback to the CAP, the result of changes in currency values, is looked upon as one of the most serious in the history of the Market. Leaders of the Six are however reasonably confident that the basic framework can be maintained. It is generally recognised as being the only way in which a fair balance can be struck between the needs of France, which has the largest agricultural sector in the Community, and the benefits which it concedes to West Germany by opening its home market to the much stronger German manufacturing industries.

It is also recognised that the framework can be used for applying common policies and payments from the common budget in other sectors, such as technology. Britain, under the entry terms, therefore eventually stands to receive substantial industrial benefits in return for the considerable sums it is expected to pay out to help French agriculture.

How will the common agricultural policy work out in practice for British farmers, food traders and consumers? Its impact will be felt in this country in four main sectors:

System of common farm prices.

Common system of protection for the Common Market against the inflow of food from external markets at prices lower than the Market's prices.

Common budget established for the Market as a whole, into which Britain will pay large sums.

Increase in Britain's food costs and therefore in the cost of living, resulting from the application in Britain of the Market's high prices.

Each of these four sectors is now analysed in detail.

The common prices system
The level of common prices in the Common Market is decided annually by the Market's Council of Ministers in which member states will, if the entry terms are implemented, be represented by their ministers of agriculture. British representatives will share responsibility with their counterparts on the Commission and CAP groups concerned with formulating price policy so that no member state suffers hardship and all have a fair share of Market benefits. The sovereignty involved in decision-making for British farms is therefore not totally handed over to Brussels. Member states reserve the right if a particular price policy does not suit them to withdraw and insist on the defence of legitimate national interests. This has been demonstrated in every year since the CAP was established at the long 'marathon' sessions required to fix farm prices.

The common pricing and related systems differ from product to product. *Cereals* are the most important products for Britain and for most of the other members, since they make up a large part of farm production and, in the form of animal foodstuffs, have an important effect on the prices of cattle (involving meat, milk, butter and cheese) and poultry (involving eggs).

The Community sets a *target price* for cereals which, as its name implies, is the price producers are intended to receive on average for their grain. It is not a guaranteed price.

The method of achieving the target price depends on maintaining a *threshold price*, below which imports from non-member countries (e.g., the Commonwealth) cannot come, and what is known as *intervention price*. This is the price at which cereal surpluses are bought in by the Community, through the common budget, to support the market.

Application of the Community policy in Britain will involve determining intervention prices in our own markets and the local pattern of intervention centres. (See British entry terms, Chapter 2, pp. 43–4.) Prices paid to British farmers will fluctuate on the basis of the threshold price (fixed for imported grain) and the intervention price (the 'floor' of the market). They vary from one member state to the other and between regions in each state, depending on local supply and demand and other factors.

Target prices are fixed annually by estimating what is a fair return for an efficient farmer in the open market in that part of the Community where cereals are in shortest supply, the town of Duisburg in West Germany. The prices, fixed for each crop year, take account of the cost of transporting cereals there. So that farmers market supplies in a regular and orderly fashion, increments are added each month to the target prices up to May (for rye, barley and maize) and to June (for wheat). For 1971–2 the target prices fixed by the Market Council were: wheat (excluding durum) £46·33 per ton; rye £42·51; barley £42·42; maize £41·02. A target price was not set for oats.

The intervention, or buying-in, price is also fixed for Duisburg and, in 1971, was about eight per cent below the target price. *Regional intervention prices* for member states are derived from the Duisburg basic intervention price and are lower to the extent that they are nearer main supply centres. Basic 1971–2 intervention prices in Duisburg were: wheat £42·64 per ton; rye £39·30; barley £38·96. These increase monthly to encourage orderly selling between September, possibly returning to original levels in June and July. Oats are not covered by intervention pricing systems and a common intervention level is established for maize in specified centres.

When cereals prices fall below the intervention price levels farmers may sell them to *national intervention agencies* on the basis of the intervention price. When surplus grain is exported to a non-member country, an *export subsidy* or *restitution* is paid to bridge the gap between Community and world prices. A subsidy is also paid if wheat is 'denatured', i.e. dyed or treated in some other way so that it is used for animal foodstuffs.

British farmers' income, when the full CAP rules apply, will therefore depend on prices fluctuating at or near the target price or the lower regional intervention price. The price levels, as explained above, ultimately depend on decisions made in Brussels by the Ministers of Agriculture of Britain and the other nine members. Precise estimates of the effect on British farm profits cannot be made because of major increases in target and intervention prices for the early and mid 1970s. Approximate figures worked out in London show that in the season 1971–2 wheat, for which the U.K. guaranteed price is £32·60 per ton, would in the Common Market rise to £41. Barley (U.K. price £29) would rise to £36; and oats (U.K. price £28·80) would rise to £34. Britain's agricultural production is expected to expand after entry, by double the rate of recent years.

For products other than cereals the CAP pricing arrangements are:

Butter, cheese and milk   A common target price has been established for milk. It is defined as the price which would give a fair return to producers for their milk delivered at the dairy, subject to market outlets being available in the Community and on the world market. The emphasis in the agreements was on price management of butter and cheese rather than on milk itself as only about a quarter of the milk produced on the farms of the Six is used for liquid consumption. The target price was maintained by means of support-buying for butter and skim milk and, in Italy, for cheese, where little butter is made. By April, 1972, a regulation for trade in liquid milk is scheduled to come into force in which there would be no official Community pricing arrangements. When high prices for dairy products led to a huge surplus of butter, the famous 'butter mountain', special subsidies were introduced under the CAP to reduce it. Grants were made to encourage the use of skim milk for animal foodstuffs and to subsidise supplies of butter at lower prices to the armed forces, schools and old people. The common budget meets these costs and also pays for giving products made from butter to developing countries. For *New Zealand butter* safeguards see Appendix 2.

Beef and veal   These were in short supply in the Six. The market organisation therefore concentrated on regulating the level of prices for importing from external markets instead of on a policy of intervention at home. A *guide price* acts as a target price and it also triggers a system of import control and intervention at home if this is required. 1971–2 guide prices: fat cattle £15·24 per live cwt.; calves £19·95.

Pigmeat (bacon and pork)   A 'floor' is maintained in the market by occasional intervention; but the policy is defined as one which establishes an intervention price which is not attractive to producers. Rather than a target price, there is a *basic price*, which works to trigger market support. The Commission decides on the level of intervention after consulting the management committee on pigs. What is called a *sluice-gate price* is fixed quarter-annually by the Commission. This is the minimum price for imports from non-member countries.

Eggs, chickens and other poultry meat   There are no arrangements for maintaining internal market prices. Imports of eggs or poultry from non-member states are at sluice-gate prices or above. If they enter below, extra levies are paid varying according to the country of origin. Sluice-gate prices are fixed on a quarterly basis and are based on the true cost of production in world markets. Variable levies are imposed above the sluice-gate prices to give Common Market producers a preference in member states.

Eggs sold in all Common Market shops are subject to strict standards regulating size and quality and there were moves made in 1971 for grading poultry meat.

Fruit and vegetables Extra responsibility is given to producer organisations for these products, resulting from the special problems raised by seasonal changes and storage. A *countervailing duty* can be imposed on imports when the import price falls below an agreed reference price on two successive days. This is in addition to customs duties. A *basic price* is calculated in member states based on the average price level of a commodity for the three previous seasons on certain markets in production areas. Member states may fix support-buying prices at between 40 and 70 per cent of the basic price. When market prices are below this buying-in price for three successive days, a state of 'serious crisis' is declared. Member governments must then intervene to restore stability. Producer organisations can fix a *reserve* or *fall-back price* for each commodity, at which price they may intervene with partial assistance of Community funds. The effect is that they do not market produce at below the reserve level.

Grading standards have been established for fruit and vegetables.

Sugar For arrangements made for U.K. and Commonwealth, see Appendix 2.

Hops No levies or refunds are provided for; imports of hops are bound in GATT with a customs duty of nine per cent. French and Belgian quota imports are due to be lifted. Grants are promised for the formation of hop producer organisations which will be concerned largely with regulating production to market needs. Subsidies, it has been stated, will be paid to hop producers if the Brussels Council of Ministers approves them on the basis of a proposal of the Commission after submission of an annual report. There are also due to be subsidies to encourage producers to change to what are considered to be better varieties of hops. The common budget would bear half the cost of these.

Of the 32-thousand acres in the Community which were growing hops, 80 per cent were in West Germany.

Mutton, lamb and potatoes The above list of products, covered by common regulations embraces 95 per cent of farm production in the Six. The only two important farming sectors, for which there were not common arrangements in 1971, are sheepmeat (mutton and lamb) and potatoes. Each of these is subject to the common external tariff which means 20 per cent on imports of mutton and lamb and 15 per cent for live sheep. *Wool* is classified by the Six as an industrial product (without support). Most imports are duty-free. Over-production of potatoes has led to pressure by some of the Six for a common organisation for them.

Wine A customs duty and variable levy system brings the price of wines imported from external markets up to Market price levels. The Six have also agreed that the strength of ordinary table wines must be between 8·5 and 15 degrees of alcohol with specifications for high quality wine and aperitifs. In the vineyards of West Germany and Luxembourg, producers may increase the alcohol content by 3·5 per cent by adding sugar because of a lack of sunshine.

Tobacco There is a common system of marketing. It was agreed that tobacco excise duties throughout the Six should be unified by 1980. France and Italy agreed to adjust their state tobacco mono-polies to Common Market rules by 1976.

The common protection system

This is the second main sector in which Britain will, if the entry terms are applied, feel the impact of the CAP. As with the common prices system, it varies from product to product. As world prices for farm products are regarded as too low to provide a standard of living for Market farmers comparable with that of factory workers, the common prices levels are much higher than prices in much of the world market.

To prevent cheap Commonwealth and other food coming into the Common Market and undercutting member states' farmers, Brussels institutions (on all of which Britain will be represented) fix a *threshold price*. This is part of the mechanism for calculating a *variable import levy*. The threshold price for cereals varies to ensure that, when it is added to the cost of transporting the goods from the seaport to Duisburg (basis of target price yardstick), the sum is equal to the Duisburg target price.

Example given by EEC officials: Assume that the Duisburg target price has been fixed at £40 a ton for a particular cereal. If the cost of transporting it from Rotterdam to Duisburg is £1 a ton the threshold price is £40 minus £1 or £39. Assume cargoes of grain are arriving at Rotterdam from non-member countries at between £20 and £25 a ton. An average is taken of the lower cost-insurance-freight (c.i.f.) prices. Assuming this is £22 the levy is the difference between it and the threshold price: £17. This is charged at all Common Market ports on that particular day. After being decided by experts from all member states the levy figure is telexed to the customs authorities in all of them so that a common barrier is simultaneously established. If the same cereal arrives the next day at lower or higher prices the levy is varied accordingly.

The common budget

This is the third and in many ways the most difficult principal sector of the CAP affecting Britain. The Six have agreed that all money paid in the form of levies on food imports into the Common Market, together with all customs duties charged on imported industrial goods plus a percentage of receipts from VAT (value-added tax) in member states, should be paid into the common budget in Brussels mainly to meet the cost of running CAP. The CAP support-buying and other costs are met by European Agricultural Guidance and Guarantee Fund (FEOGA—the initials of its name in French). The guidance part of its title refers to money paid to member states for reforming the structure of Common Market agricultures, i.e. to supplement the money they spend on modernising their farms at the national level.

It is the guarantee section of FEOGA which meets the costs of support-buying and helps with denaturing food to be used for animal feeding. It also pays what are called *export refunds* (restitutions or subsidies) on Common Market foodstuffs which are exported to the external markets. When world prices are lower than the Market prices, the refund is paid to make up the difference so that the Market food exporter receives, in all, the same price for his exports outside the Market as he does inside it.

As Britain and West Germany are major food importers and have relatively little food to spare for exports, the CAP protection and budget rules mean they will pay by the 1980s the largest part of farm costs through the common budget. This raised the most difficult problem in the entry negotiations. Not only is Britain's bill high but, as her agriculture is efficient, she stands to receive very little from the budget for modernising her farms.

The application of the CAP rules to our farmers will be implemented under the auspices of British agricultural officials. Under terms worked out by Geoffrey Rippon and Freddie Kearns of the Ministry of Agriculture, it has been agreed that there will be an annual review in which the British minister of agriculture will consult the farmers on their needs. British farmers will also be able to exert pressure on the Brussels institutions through COPA, the powerful European equivalent of the National Farmers Union.

France, which stands to gain so much from the enlarged common agricultural market in extra sales of her produce to Britain, tried to force the negotiators to agree to full application of CAP rules to British farms soon after entry into the Market. In fact, Britain will be allowed five years.

Increase in food prices

The first upward movement of food prices in Britain, resulting from the CAP to bring them into line with high price levels in the Market, will not take place until late 1973. On that date, the gap between farm prices in Britain and the Six will be narrowed by 16·6 per cent. It will be narrowed by four further cuts of 16·6 per cent on July 1 of each subsequent year until disappearing on December 31, 1977, with a final cut of 16·6 per cent.

The British government estimated in 1971 that entry would affect food prices in Britain gradually with an increase of about 2·5 per cent each year in retail prices, which will continue to be fixed by officials here. As food absorbs about a quarter of total consumer expenditure, the effect on the cost of living was estimated at about 0·5 per cent per year.

Butter, beef and cheese were expected to rise by the late 1970s by more than the average; bread, flour and eggs by about the average; and milk, fish, oils and fats, tea and coffee were not expected to show much change. For some fruit and vegetables, prices might go lower at certain times of the year. These estimates sharply contrasted with those which forecast an 18–26 per cent jump in food prices in the Labour Government White Paper in 1970. After that, however, the gap between British and Common Market food prices substantially narrowed, partly the result of an increase in world prices and partly of rising prices in Britain.

During the period from 1973 to 1977 when Britain will be raising its farm prices to the levels of the Six it will also gradually open up its 'home' market to produce from the Market member states and move up to the common levy of the Six towards the rest of the world.

At first Britain will introduce its own threshold and intervention prices. These will be lower than the full Common Market threshold and intervention prices referred to above. The difference, as the 1971 White Paper explains, corresponds to the difference between our market price levels and those of the Six. France and the rest of the Six will enjoy what is called *community preference* immediately, an arrangement enabling Community grown produce to sell on the British market more cheaply than produce from the Commonwealth or other suppliers with the exception of New Zealand dairy products and sugar from the developing Commonwealth.

There will be free trade with the Six in farm products covered by the CAP, subject from 1973 to 1978 only to arrangements to compensate for the difference in price levels. These arrangements take the form of fixed levies on our exports to them and fixed compensatory payments on their exports to us. The levies and export payments will gradually be reduced by the six steps over five years. On price increase adjustments, a 20 per cent flexibility margin is allowed.

TIME-TABLE FOR RAISING AGRICULTURAL PRICES IN BRITAIN TO COMMON MARKET LEVELS

	Increase	Percentage of price gap
July 1, 1973	16·6% (of price gap)	16·6%
July 1, 1974	16·6%	33·3%
July 1, 1975	16·6%	49·9%
July 1, 1976	16·6%	66·6%
July 1, 1977	16·6%	83·3%
December 12, 1977	16·6%	100%

These figures are percentages of the gap between British and Common Market prices at the beginning of 1973. In some cases the actual month in which the change is made will vary according to the commodity and the date of the beginning of the crop year. The table does not apply to horticulture.

For those agricultural commodities for which the Common Market has a common external tariff (CET) instead of, or in addition to, levies, the adjustments in Britain to that tariff will be similar to those agreed upon for industrial goods. There would be a 40 per cent movement to the CET on January 1, 1974, and three subsequent annual movements of 20 per cent to complete the alignment by July 1, 1977.

For Ireland and the other two applicants for membership, Norway and Denmark, there will be arrangements for adjusting their farm prices to Common Market levels similar to those for Britain. The arrangements will also be extended to trade between the applicants. The expert view in Brussels is that Ireland should benefit considerably from outlets in the enlarged Common Market for its meat and dairy products. As it has so much grass for feeding its cattle it will not have to buy large quantities of animal foodstuffs at the higher Market prices.

PROSPECTS FOR BRITISH FARMERS

New opportunities for many branches of British farming will undoubtedly be provided when the country becomes a member of the

Common Market. The industry will begin with the great advantage that, since the Second World War, it has become one of the most efficient in the world. Britain's farmers have more than doubled their output in 30 years, despite less manpower and land, and now produce two-thirds of the food needed by an increased population if tropical and sub-tropical products are excluded. Yet 50 years ago the United Kingdom was only 40 per cent self-sufficient in food.

How does British agriculture compare with that of the present European Economic Community countries and the other three nations which will be joining with it? The answer must be extremely favourably. Farms in the EEC are very small compared with those in Britain. The average size is only 30 acres compared with 80 acres in the United Kingdom. And in the Common Market labour productivity is lower, with the ratio of farmworkers to farmers two-to-one, considered against one-to-one in the United Kingdom.

While time and government measures have largely sorted out Britain's farm structure problems, the situation in the EEC is still causing major difficulties for reformers. Only ten per cent of a total of nearly five-million farms in the Community are up to modern standards of management and economic efficiency while 2·5-million units are run by ageing farmers, 75 per cent of whom have no potential successor.

So British agriculture stands poised not only to consolidate and increase its share of the home market, but to seize the opportunities which an enlarged market of 255-million will present. The National Farmers Union of England and Wales, which canvassed the view of its 59 county branches on the attitude of its 180-thousand members to the decision to join the Common Market, says: 'The resolutions received from county branches indicate that members broadly endorse the initial judgment by the union's council that for the industry as a whole the terms of entry should provide producers over the years ahead with opportunities to increase their production and incomes.' With the right policies and confidence there is little doubt, the union says, that by the end of the transitional period producers could achieve a government forecast of an additional eight per cent in output over and above the expansion that would otherwise have been expected. The total extra production would, it is estimated, result in an extra net saving of imports worth £350-million to £400-million per annum.

In considering the opportunities for selling farm produce in a greatly enlarged market, another factor is that British farmers will also receive a much higher price for a number of things they produce.

Cereal growers and beef producers in particular should benefit from the much higher prices which they will receive after entry. There should be big opportunities for increased beef production with a deficit of over ten per cent inside the present Common Market. Our own production, showing a welcome increase, is forecast at 75 per cent of total supply for 1970–71, and with imports from the Irish Republic, Britain could be self-sufficient in fresh meat and in the years ahead even be able to send some of its high quality beef to the other countries of the Ten. But, with increasing cereal costs, more emphasis will have to be put on grass as a cheap form of animal feeding. This will probably mean greater concentration of prime beef raising in the traditional livestock areas of the western part of Britain, leaving cereals largely to the areas of the country where they can be best grown.

There will undoubtedly be big opportunities in the enlarged Common Market for British flockmasters. Britain has as many sheep as all the present Common Market countries put together, and, while British mutton and lamb have not prominently figured among the roasts on Continental tables, there are now signs of a growing demand. France is the only member state paying much attention to the possibilities presented by this increased interest in quality lamb in the Common Market, and it is a compliment to British flockmasters that it is looking to breeds originally introduced from Britain to provide it with much of the increased production at which it is aiming.

The Market will be wide open to British sheep men, long experienced in serving the British market. Already there are signs that sheep production, long in a decline in Britain, is gaining popularity with better home prices. There should not only be room in the British market for mutton and lamb produced at home, which now accounts for only some 40 per cent of total supply, but also for a continuation of a great deal of the vast quantity we now import from New Zealand. With New Zealand supplies dovetailing into our own, serving the British market when domestic lamb becomes scarce, there should be a major increase in exports to the Continent when native lambs become available. But it is essential that in considering increased exports more attention should be paid to presentation.

As to wool, it is treated in the present Common Market as an industrial raw material and is imported duty-free. The British Wool Marketing Board will doubtless be looking for increased outlets for British wool to sell more than present quantities. More will be available with the greater numbers of sheep on British farms.

British pig producers, and the same also applies to poultry

producers, are more likely to continue supplying the home market. The Ten, like the Six, would be self-sufficient and the industries will be faced with higher prices for feed as a result of the increased cereal prices. But these sections of British farming, particularly the poultry industry, are highly efficient. Poultry farming is already mostly done in large units. The pig industry will probably move towards larger units but its main competitors for the British bacon market, for which it is steadily winning a greater share, will continue to be Denmark, a partner in the enlarged Community, which will be looking for increased markets for pork in Germany and other Common Market countries. Ireland and the Netherlands, at present supplying the British market with smaller quantities of bacon, would have free entry to our market as members of the Community.

Britain's efficient chicken and turkey producers will have no difficulty in maintaining their grip on the British market. Home production of poultry meat at 570-thousand tons accounts for virtually all of the home market, and it can be quickly increased to take advantage of new trade in Germany.

Milk producers, with their unique main market for liquid milk, will benefit from the higher EEC milk prices. In Common Market countries, where the emphasis is on milk for manufacture, 80 per cent is processed. In Britain, where the housewife has the advantage of a doorstep service, milk tankers from the Continent are not considered a serious threat. Producers will not only benefit from a higher milk price, but will get higher prices for their calves bought for replacements and beef production and for cull cows. More emphasis is likely to be placed on cheaper summer production from grass, to counteract higher costs for winter feed. The Milk Marketing Board, as well as other similar boards in Britain, should also be able to continue full operations inside the enlarged Community.

The government has already stated confidence in Britain's ability, as a member of the enlarged Community, to deal with the special conditions which farmers in the hill areas, the reservoir of our store livestock, have to face.

There should be increased trade for British processed food which already has a sizable market on the Continent. We already have exports of food and feedingstuffs to the rest of the enlarged Community worth around £100-million a year, and the Minister of Agriculture, James Prior, has said that the attractiveness of this market will increase as the levies charged by the present Community are progressively reduced and Britain gains preference over third suppliers.

Most of the criticism of the Common Market has been aimed at the common agricultural policy. Its main disadvantages for Britain arise from the fact that it was designed for six countries which struck what they regarded as a fair balance of profit and loss for them. If Britain had responded in the 1950s to the invitation of the Six to join them in forming the Market, its interests would have been safeguarded from the beginning. It is, say the Six, now too late to make fundamental changes in the CAP framework solely to suit newcomers.

It is maintained, however, that no member state need fear that it will be forced to accept serious damage to its vital interests in the agricultural or any other field. It was established during the entry negotiations that if, because of the CAP costs or for any other reason, a country's interests were to be seriously threatened, action would be taken to meet the problem. All member states can be relied on to fulfil this undertaking because each of them has a direct interest in ensuring the stability of the system.

The Commission has considerable freedom to act independently in some areas of farm policy as a result of powers delegated to it by the Ministerial Council. In practice, however, the head of the common agricultural system, Sicco Mansholt, takes the greatest care to ensure full consultation with national governments. This consultation with ministers of member states and their civil servants begins long before a Commission decision is made. In addition, there are provisions for close contact at every stage with representatives of the farmers. After the Commission has decided to initiate proposals before the Council, draft proposals are first prepared by a working party of officials from member states. Consultations are held at Community level with the liaison committees of national producers and trade interests. When the Commission has drawn up its proposals it submits these to the Council which consults the European Parliament and the Economic and Social Committee (representatives of trade unions, employers and professional bodies). Any remaining difficulties are considered by the most important of the Council's expert committees, notably the Special Committee for Agriculture, comprising senior officials of member states, which prepares most of the agricultural business for the Council. The Committee of Permanent Representatives (ambassadors of member states) is concerned with such things as finance.

The ultimate safeguard for national governments comes when the Council receives the proposals and ministers can exercise a veto. On most matters, however, ministers are able to reach workable compromises. Management committees for each group of farm products help with the Commission's day-to-day decisions on the running of the CAP. Each committee consists of officials from the national ministries of agriculture and, usually, representatives of national marketing organisations, all of whom are responsible to their own governments. An official of the Commission acts as chairman. Voting on the committee is weighted so that the larger countries have more votes than the smaller ones.

If, for instance, the Commission decides to change the import levy on pigmeat, it puts the proposal before the management committee which deals with pigmeat production. Under the system operated by the Six, France, Italy and West Germany have four votes each, Belgium and Holland two votes, and Luxembourg one. The majority voting system is used. If 12 of the 17 votes are in favour of the proposal it is applied. If the voting goes against the proposal, the Commission can still apply the proposal but the Council of Ministers can, if it acts within one month, reject it or change it. Britain will have representatives on these committees, with the same voting powers as France, Italy and West Germany.

Observers are generally agreed that the basic system of common protection operating in Brussels is as good as our deficiency payments system, which in any case could not be applied in the Market because it would be too costly and would raise acute administrative problems.

What matters most is the manner in which the common protection system is run. There has been sharp criticism of some of the Brussels decisions affecting trade relations with countries outside the Six. Officials in other countries have pointed out that decisions made to reduce the Market's 'butter mountain', with the help of export refunds, meant that butter from the Six was dumped all over the world in ways gravely threatening the interests of other producers. Fortunately, a drought resulted in a butter shortage and this reduced the damage to world trade.

Some decisions fixing the import levies for cereals have, in the opinion of some non-member countries raised unnecessary difficulties. An example is given of a cargo of grain from the outside world which, when it began its long journey to Europe, appeared likely to be sold at a reasonable price in the Market. Just as the grain was arriving at Rotterdam a low-priced cereals offer received by the Market officials triggered off a levy which meant an absurdly low selling price. Such decisions have led to allegations that the Six are too 'inward-looking'. There have also been cases of illegal use of the protection mechanisms. British entry, say the Six, may lead to a tightening up of the methods for implementing policies.

The fact that the Six have managed to complete the CAP despite major crises, some of which brought the whole Market to the brink of collapse, is proof of their political will to unite Western Europe. Many of their leaders, notably Dr. Mansholt, look upon the CAP not only as an instrument for helping farmers but as part of the cement holding the European Community together. Without the CAP, France, particularly in the early Gaullist era, might well have abandoned the Market. One of the first problems to be tackled on British entry arises from the Commission's plans for heavy expenditure on measures to persuade more farmers to leave the land. As Britain shoulders a major part of the farm budget these plans will be closely scrutinised in Whitehall. Some of the Six have argued that it is better for Britain to face a heavier charge in the short term to reduce the farm population to assure big reductions in the cost of farm surpluses in the long term. British officials have not been convinced.

In the long term, the success of the CAP will largely depend on the extent to which the ten members of the enlarged Common Market can stabilise their currencies thus making it possible to remove the barriers which have been temporarily applied by the Six against the free flow of farm goods between them. Some Germans have urged that the barriers should become permanent and this has led to fears that the agricultures of the member states might be 're-nationalised'.

The Commission and some member states stress that the only lasting solutions in the agricultural sectors can be found by fully implementing the plans for economic and monetary union which aim at stabilising and eventually unifying the Market's currencies. This is another example of the pragmatic philosophy of the founders in action that 'integration in one field must lead eventually to integration in other and perhaps in all fields'.

An important issue facing the Ten is: should they hurry on towards full economic and ultimately full monetary union or should they allow key sectors of the Market's existing integration to stagnate and perhaps disintegrate? The policies and prospects of the proposed economic and monetary union are described in the next chapter.

BRITISH HORTICULTURE

For British horticulture the national tariff, which has been its main form of protection, will be reduced between Britain and the other members of the enlarged Common Market at a slower rate than the one fixed for agricultural and industrial tariffs.

The national tariff will remain unchanged in the first year, 1973,

100 THE COMMON AGRICULTURAL MARKET

after entry. Horticulturists of the Six and the other applicants will have free access to the British market by 1978.

Britain's import quotas on apples and pears will be replaced, under the entry terms, by compensatory import levies offsetting the difference between British and Community prices. These levies will be phased out over five years to bring prices gradually into line, with a percentage of tolerance up or down for flexibility.

The British horticultural industry is subject to some climatic and structural disadvantages. There are, however, some sectors in which it is competitive. The Government White Paper says that in all sectors there will be opportunities for efficient growers. For apple and pear growers, however, it will be difficult.

Expansion of fruit production in the Common Market over the last 15 years, especially in France and Italy, is such that a million tons surplus of apples is expected by 1975. What can British growers do to meet the free access to their market which France and Italy will have? Cox's Orange Pippin and other leading varieties which most people in this country prefer to the Continental Golden Delicious dessert apple, should maintain their competitive ability. The British glasshouse producers will face competition from outdoor tomatoes grown in southern France and Italy, but 40 per cent of British horticultural production is in field vegetables for the home market and should not be affected.

Assistance for new investment is already given under the horticulture improvement scheme in Britain and the government announced a high rate of grant for grubbing up old orchards to improve the market for commercial producers. When efficient growers face special problems of adjustment they will be given the necessary help to meet them. Packaging, presentation and organisation of market will be important.

It is also agreed that the enlarged Common Market would be ready to take prompt and effective action to deal with difficulties arising out of the transitional arrangements for horticulture.

COMMON FISHERIES MARKET

The Common Market fisheries policy, intended to allow all member states free-for-all fishing to each other's beaches, will not come into effect in Britain for ten years after entry. Before the end of that period (January 1983) the Brussels institutions will review the situation.

If at that time it is clear that British fishermen are as dependent on inshore fishing as they are now, and that application of the policy would seriously reduce fish stocks, these factors will be taken fully into account in the review. Britain, with the support of other member countries for which fisheries are important, would then insist that the application of the policy be again delayed or that the policy itself be changed. Meanwhile Britain will continue in full control of the six-mile zone and, in important areas, will control up to 12 miles. This is the core of the fisheries terms negotiated by Mr. Rippon in December 1971 after wrangling among the four applicants and between them and the Six extending over six months.

The common fisheries policy of the Six, which by a 'curious coincidence' (Mr. Rippon's words) was completed just as full-scale negotiations were opening with Britain in June 1970, calls for a free market for fish throughout the Community. The Six agreed that full access for each other's fishing vessels up to their beaches would be allowed in the mid 1970s. Price arrangements would vary according to the kind of fish. There would be a *guide price* for fresh fish based on market prices for the previous three years. This price would guide producer organisations. It was laid down that they should withdraw fish from the market at between 60 and 90 per cent of the guide price.

Part One of the agreed text of the British fisheries agreement says that: 'the member states of the enlarged Community shall be authorised until December 31, 1982, to restrict fishing in waters under their sovereignty or jurisdiction, situated within a limit of six nautical miles—calculated from the base lines of the coastal member states—to vessels based on ports in the same geographical coastal area and which fish traditionally in those waters'. (A base line is one drawn between headlands.)

Part Two of the agreed text of the fisheries terms says that the six mile limit will be extended to twelve miles in the following areas of Britain and Ireland:

United Kingdom:
   Shetland and Orkney Islands.
   North and East Scotland: from Cape Wrath round the north-eastern part of Scotland and along the whole of Scotland's eastern coast down to Berwick.
   North East England: from the River Coquet, north of Newcastle, to Flamborough Head (from Flamborough Head, the rest of the east coast of England, the south east and the south of England up to Lyme Regis will not be under control beyond the six-mile limit).
   South West England: from Lyme Regis round to Hartland Point (including 12 miles surrounding Lundy Island).
   There will be control up to the six-mile limit for Wales and North West England.
   County Down: controlled 12-mile limit throughout its coastal waters.
   West Coast of Scotland: the agreed text does not refer directly to this coast but makes it clear that the control continues up to six miles. As these are measured

from base lines, control in fact extends throughout the whole of the Minches which will therefore be free from foreign fishermen. The Hebrides and other nearby islands will also be covered by the six-mile limit control.

Ireland: the coasts north and west of Lough Foyle as far as Cork in the South West; the coast east of Dundalk Bay as far as Carnsore Point for fisheries of crustaceans and shellfish. (Ireland also accepted that the review clause applied to Britain's fisheries should also apply to Ireland's after the ten-year period.)

National measures of conservation may be maintained within the 12-mile limit over which full jurisdiction is maintained as long as these measures are non-discriminatory.

Part Three of the fisheries terms is concerned with ensuring protection of *deep sea waters* and the preservation of *biological resources* of the sea.

Part Four says: 'Before December 31, 1982, the Commission will present to the Council a report concerning the *economic and social development* of the coastal areas of the member states and the state of stocks. On the basis of this report, and of the objectives of the common fisheries policy of the Community, the Council, acting on a proposal of the Commission, will examine the arrangements which could follow the derogations in force until December 31, 1982.

6

TOWARDS A COMMON CURRENCY

Since 1968 the Common Market has been a free trade area in which no tariffs or customs duties are levied on manufactured goods or foodstuffs passing from one member country to another. But it will not be a fully unified market in which completely free competition applies for manufacturers and farmers until all economic policies have been standardised. In particular, Europe will require a single currency before it can be truly described as an integrated market.

Until that day the value of individual member states' currencies will tend to vary, appreciating and depreciating in purchasing power in relation to the rate at which prices change. Countries with under-valued currencies which have suffered from rapid inflation will find exporting difficult and find foreign goods relatively cheaper than their own. These conditions may have to be corrected by devaluations and revaluations which will change business costs and affect the relative costs of raw materials and finished goods.

Once a unified currency has been achieved, nullifying the ability to revalue or devalue, rapidly rising wages and other costs in one of the member states will lead to falling profitability, bankruptcies and rising unemployment, without an opportunity for a national government to correct the imbalance by altering the exchange rate. If corporation taxes and regional incentive premiums are harmonised and centrally regulated, there will be no escape from the consequence of excessive rates of inflation in different parts of the Community.

Wages increases will have to be regulated within the capacity of businesses to pay them. It will only be feasible to increase incomes once productivity of labour can be improved and management can devise more efficient methods.

Integration of economic policies is essential if currency crises are to be avoided in future, competition is to be fully effective, and the common farm policy is to work effectively. Different economic policies in the individual member states were responsible for currencies getting out of alignment; devaluation of the French franc and revaluation of the mark in 1969, and the floating of the mark and the guilder in 1971, damaged the implementation of the farm price policy which was only preserved by the introduction of complicated bridging regulations.

It has become clear that economic policies can only be integrated by planning a new stage of development of the Community leading to standardised policies for competition and economic growth and a common currency. The administration of these new policies would also require a substantial increase in the powers of the Common Market Commission in Brussels.

In December, 1969, the Six decided at a meeting in The Hague to accelerate their progress towards economic and monetary union. In February, 1970, the Community established a 2,000-million dollar fund to provide help for member states with currencies victimised by speculation, and to inform each other of any drastic plans which would affect the economies of other members. In February, 1971, the Six adopted a three-stage plan for complete economic and monetary union by the end of 1980.

By the end of 1973 members will take fundamental political decisions about the ultimate shape of the Community and decide whether to transfer gradually sovereignty over economic policy away from the member governments to institutions in Brussels and the European Parliament in Strasbourg.

The effective devaluation of the dollar and upward valuation *inter alia* of the Deutsche Mark, the Dutch guilder and the Belgian franc in December 1971, ended the dollar's post-war supremacy as the international currency. It opens the way for developing a European currency system and eventually a united currency which will be on an equal footing with the dollar.

Progress was halted by the currency crisis in May 1971, but attempts have already been made to continue towards monetary integration. British goods, as a result of currency realignments, will be slightly cheaper in Germany, the Netherlands, Belgium and Luxembourg, but significantly more expensive in the U.S., South Africa, India and East and West Africa.

There is no reason to believe that the obligations of moving towards monetary union as and when they are decided should be particularly onerous for the United Kingdom. If British labour and management interests can adopt the necessary flexibility there is good reason to believe that economic union will enable the British economy to grow as fast as that of the Community as a whole. On the record of the past 15 years that would require the British economy to grow at a faster rate than it would otherwise do.

Regional development policies exist inside the Community and substantial help would be available from its institutions to help the economic redevelopment of regions with declining industries and remote agricultural areas such as the hill farming districts of Wales and the Highlands and Islands of Scotland. The Community's regional policies include: establishment of development plans; creation of an interest-rebate fund for regional development financed from budgetary contributions and administered by the Commission; a guarantee system for regional development, the cost of which is to be shared out among the member governments.

Grants are also available from the European Agricultural Fund for structural improvements in farming. Investment projects can also be financed by the European Investment Bank, Social Fund and European Coal and Steel Community readaptation grants to retrain and resettle workers. The ECSC also offers loans to attract new industries to areas where traditional industries of coal and iron are in decline.

Britain will have to wind up the functions of sterling as a reserve currency as part of the understanding reached in Paris between President Pompidou and Prime Minister Heath. The terms of the agreement pledge Britain to reduce, wherever possible, the amount of sterling owned by member governments of the sterling area. The first steps to this end were taken in September, 1971, when the minimum proportion of reserves these countries were required to hold in sterling was reduced across the board by ten per cent.

At some stage in the future the sterling involved will presumably be redeemed by Britain in exchange for its share of some future issue of special drawing rights by the International Monetary Fund.

Balance of Payments
For the effect on Britain's balance of payments resulting from contributions to the common budget under the agricultural policy, see Appendix, p. 179.

Capital Movements
Of the three basic objectives of the Rome treaty, freedom of trade, labour and capital movement, progress has been slowest in relaxing controls on capital. This is not surprising in view of the balance of payments difficulties of various members from time to time. It was in fact the economic problems confronting France when the Treaty of Rome was drafted that led to the vagueness in the wording of Articles 67–73 which embody the provisions relating to freedom of capital movements.

ARTICLE 67 requires member states to abolish progressively restrictions on capital movements between each other and to abolish discrimination based on nationality or place of residence or where the capital was invested, provided that ultimate ownership lies in an EEC member state. Unlike the forthright measures liberalising trade and labour movements, this article need be implemented only to the extent 'necessary for the proper functioning of the Common Market'. Furthermore, no time-table was laid down for freeing capital flows.

ARTICLE 68 requires members to be as liberal as possible in granting whatever exchange authorisations are still necessary after the inception of the Treaty.

ARTICLE 69 permits the Council of Ministers to issue directives to implement the liberalisation measures. In the early stages, complete unanimity is required, with qualified majority voting coming into operation at the final stage. The intransigent French attitude to majority voting has made it unlikely so far that any attempt will be made to impose a decision on an unwilling state.

ARTICLE 70 provides for co-ordination between member states in their dealings with third countries on capital movements.

ARTICLE 71 prevents members from introducing new exchange regulations or from making existing regulations more restrictive.

ARTICLE 72 obliges members to inform the Commission on all known capital movements with third countries and permits the Commission to comment as it thinks fit.

ARTICLE 73 is an escape clause dealing with capital movements which cause a disturbance in the operation of any member's domestic capital market. Following consultation with the Monetary Committee, the Commission can authorise the member state to take protective measures and determine the conditions or details. In cases of urgency, a member state may take such measures independently or without prior consultation. In such an event, the Commission would have to be informed as soon as the measures come into effect, and after consultation, the member can be required to modify or remove the measures.

Since the Treaty became effective, there have been two directives on capital movements (1960 and 1962) and an unsuccessful attempt to introduce a third directive (1967). In essence, the first two directives divided capital transactions into four categories and established different rules for each sector.

The first two categories were freed from all restrictions. They include direct investments, listed securities, personal capital movements (e.g. insurance payments, immigrants' remittances), payments on property transactions and short- and medium-term credits for commercial transactions or service payments.

The third category consists of dealings which member states may govern by regulations 'if those movements are such as to impede the achievement of the objectives of their policy'. Transactions in this category include the issue of foreign securities on capital markets, and financial loans and credits to borrowers in other Community countries. Of the member states, Germany, Belgium and Luxembourg had relaxed restrictions prior to the issue of the Directive and cannot impose new regulations unless they invoke the 'escape clause'. France, Italy and the Netherlands took advantage of the rules to uphold partial restrictions on such capital movements.

The fourth category consists of a brief list of miscellaneous transactions such as overseas deposits, for which no special rules were formulated.

It should be stressed that the Directives establish minimum requirements: member states can and do liberate capital movements over and above the requirements of the Directives.

The conflict over the 1967 proposed Directive arose over measures to harmonise certain aspects of the international capital market which were causing anomalies. In particular, the Commission wanted to eliminate double taxation on income from securities or on loan interest transferred from one member state to another. A further Draft Directive on this topic was tabled to the Council of Ministers in 1969.

At the same time, a second Draft Directive sought to revise current tax regulations which constitute a major obstacle to mergers across Community frontiers. Such mergers often give rise to untaxed (unrealised) capital gains resulting from a difference between the book values and real values of the assets acquired. Preferential treatment is often given to domestic mergers but not to take-overs by companies in other Community countries.

The Commission's proposal to deal with this situation is that no tax should become payable until or unless undisclosed assets revealed by a trans-national merger are converted into cash. Equally, reserves built up for specific commercial requirements should remain tax free.

More recently, considerable strain has been placed on the concept of freedom of capital movement by the international currency crisis. In particular, the central banks of the Six, acting in a wider context, moved to curb speculative or non-commercial flows of currency, in particular, of Euro-dollars. Catching up with events, the Commission recognised the need for certain member states (notably Germany) to supplement their exchange control systems even when this involved a retreat from the Directives already adopted.

According to the International Monetary Fund, Britain has equipped itself with one of the most complex and far-reaching systems of exchange control in the world. The principal fears of British authorities in adopting the capital movements provisions are that there would be an excessive outflow of investment capital into Europe and of portfolio capital into the U.S. as a result of relaxing Britain's exchange control structure.

The British have reached agreement with the Community on a three-phase time-table:

1. A two-year period for the relaxation of controls on direct investments in Community countries, according to the categories established in the 1960 and 1962 Directives.
2. A period of two and a half years for the liberation of personal capital movements.
3. For portfolio investment, liberation would be fully established by the end of the five-year transitional period.

Britain has conceded that the relaxation process could be speeded up if the balance of payments remains sufficiently strong to cope with such an acceleration. It has also clarified the position by indicating that restriction would be abolished, from the date of membership, on the transfer of credits relating to trade and services which do not constitute a direct investment abroad. In the case of direct investment, controls are to be relaxed in two stages: the first on membership and the second after two years.

On the question of the freedom of transferability of personal capital, the Treasury's insistence on a delay until the middle of the transitional period stems from the fear that substantial sums owned by people retiring abroad would be moved out of the country immediately. Currently, people retiring abroad from Britain may take only £5,000 with them, any other funds being frozen for four years. No obstacle would be placed in the way of anyone wishing to transfer personal funds abroad if they were moving to 'exercise economic activity'.

The implications for Britain of easing exchange control regulations are difficult to assess, partly because tight controls have been in force since the beginning of the Second World War. In view of the history of panic flights from sterling in the past, British officials have been apprehensive about the possible effects of exchange control relaxation. The questions of the sterling area and the role of sterling as a reserve currency are being treated as a general problem affecting the entire Community.

On portfolio investment, it is likely that the British government will seek to maintain a barrier against free investment in non-Community stock markets. The situation is fluid because the Community has yet to agree upon a common policy on external portfolio investment. Britain as a member of the Community would obviously play a part in formulating common rules—and it might be possible for it to make it difficult for investors to transfer liquid funds to areas of member states whose attitude to external investment has been more liberal.

Euro Property

There is a striking contrast between the basic structure of the residential property market in this country and that of the six original members of the EEC. It is explained by the relative scarcity of land in Britain which has lead to a constant pressure on property prices unknown in Europe, together with a more sophisticated approach to the property market.

In addition, differences in the composition of towns and cities on the Continent and in the way of life of people has led the vast majority to house themselves in flats. In France in 1970, only 33·9 per cent of homes were individual houses and only 25 per cent of homes constructed were homes for one family.

Not all the Six are as popular as countries such as Spain and Portugal for the British property buyer looking for a house in Europe. This may change in future. Many more British residents will be considering the purchase of a property abroad, whether from necessity of business or out of choice as a holiday or retirement retreat.

At present, Bank of England regulations allow each family to buy one residence outside the sterling area. Before doing so, it is obligatory to obtain the Bank's permission. Unlike buying a house within the sterling area, in Malta or Cyprus for example, the exchange control regulations stipulate that the deal must be carried through in dollars bought from the Dollar/Property Investment 'pool'. The purchaser pays a premium on the amount required because demand normally exceeds supply: the premium has been as high as 60 per cent. It now stands at around 20 per cent. If he were buying a house of about £10,000 and the dollar premium was standing at 20 per cent, the buyer would have to pay £12,000 for the privilege of moving the money for the house out of this country. If he were subsequently to sell the house, he would have the sale price returned, including the premium.

British membership in the Common Market does not significantly alter this position because the process of financial integration is being undertaken very slowly. Thus the premium is likely to remain for some time. It will probably only begin to be phased out towards the end of the five-year transitional period from 1973. Only when the dollar premium has been abandoned, will it be possible to say that buying property inside the Community may have clear financial advantages over buying in the sterling area or elsewhere.

This country enjoys the most developed system of home loans in the world, thanks to the building society movement. In Europe the loans are smaller, for shorter periods and at higher rates of interest. Such loans that are available cannot in fact be used by British residents. Thus, buying a house in Europe will still mean finding the full amount in cash for the majority.

Many live abroad during their retirement, therefore tax plays an important part in their choice of country. In France for instance a British non-resident does not pay French income tax but is subject to the U.K. non-residents tax. This situation will continue to prevail until this country is finally integrated into Europe during the late 1970s. Probably the two easiest cities for businessmen are Brussels and Amsterdam. Both have had much recent property development and the market is more open. The Dutch, in particular, have a superior mortgage system.

Finally, the legal differences between Britain and Europe, typified by the Code Napoleon, are considerable. Transfer charges do not compare favourably: $2\frac{1}{2}$ per cent here compared with up to 10 per cent in some member countries. It is of the utmost importance that prospective purchasers deal with a reputable estate agent with experience in Europe, of whom there are already several.

Value-Added Tax

The value-added tax is the most distinctive feature of taxation in the EEC. It is the basic method of indirect taxation throughout the Community, and is paid by every manufacturer and service industry on the difference between the cost of materials and labour and the selling price of his product. As such, it is a rather complicated tax to calculate and requires every commercial business throughout the Community to keep detailed records of purchases and sales. It becomes even more complicated when different types of items are taxed at different rates. Studies on the effect of introducing a VAT in Britain have suggested it could cost up to £20-million a year and require several thousand more civil servants to administer it.

It has the advantage of being broadly based, including all levels of manufacturing and service industries. Consequently it is less arbitrary than purchase tax and the individual rates of tax need not be so high because the range of items is larger. Although it is paid at all stages of production, every time materials are processed and sold right up to the final article, nothing is taxed twice, because the tax already paid on materials is deducted from the tax on the resale price of the goods manufactured at each stage. The tax can also be repaid in full to exporters who can thus market goods more cheaply abroad. Although British exports are also exempt from purchase tax, it is calculated that nearly a fifth of the purchase tax paid on components is not rebated because the amounts cannot be calculated.

Two or three rates of VAT are practical, and certain items such as foodstuffs can be exempt altogether. A zero rate will almost certainly be charged on food and items, such as fertilizers, bought by farmers. The attractions of VAT in Britain are that relatively low rates will be possible on items, such as cars and consumer durables, which in the past have carried a high level of purchase tax. Even modest rates of tax, including a zero rate and perhaps a $7\frac{1}{2}$ and 15 per cent rate would yield enough revenue to replace purchase tax and the widely disliked selective employment tax.

Although Britain will be obliged as a member of EEC to adopt a VAT, individual rates will be allowed to vary from country to country for the forseeable future. Eventually, however, the rates will be brought into line throughout the Community and goods will be able to cross internal borders without being subject to refunds of the exporting country's VAT. Britain introduces it in April, 1973.

At a still later stage excise duties on petrol, alcohol and tobacco will be standardised. This could mean lower excise duties in the U.K. Corporation taxes will also have to be harmonised at some stage, so that economic conditions become as similar as possible in all parts of the Community and fair competition can be encouraged. It is also intended to encourage mergers between companies in different countries in order to allow for the development of companies capable of competing with American rivals. Special incentives will continue to operate in regions of high unemployment, but these incentives will also have to be standardised.

Double taxation on dividends will also be eliminated. Taxes on the raising of capital were generally standardised in 1969. There are, however, no plans at this stage to try and harmonise income taxes in all the member states, because this tax does not affect business conditions. As a result, income tax policy will remain a powerful instrument in the hands of individual governments until such time as political integration is achieved.

Commercial Policy
The EEC has been a major power in international trade almost from its outset. Although trade between members has grown particularly

quickly, EEC exports and imports to and from third countries have also risen steadily. The Community became the world's largest trading block in the late 1960s when its exports to third countries overtook exports of the U.S.

The Community negotiated as a single unit in the Kennedy Round talks on tariff reductions from 1965 to 1967, even before the common external tariff (CET) was introduced on July 1, 1968. On that date, all import duties on goods coming from outside the Community were standardised. In December, 1969, the Six agreed that all non-member states wishing to negotiate a trade agreement with the Community would have to negotiate with the Community rather than with individual members.

After the end of 1972, even the residual rights of member states to negotiate bilateral trade agreements with countries which do not recognise the Community, specifically the Soviet Union and the countries of Eastern Europe, will disappear and the external trade policies of the member states will be standardised completely. All negotiations will then be handled by the Commission in Brussels. In 1968, the Community adopted measures to co-ordinate anti-dumping policies in the member countries. The next year, individual national import quotas were co-ordinated and Community quotas set, to be allocated among member states.

The Community has also taken a consistent attitude towards its trade relations with less developed countries, adopting a common policy with respect to non-reciprocal preferences to be given to imports of manufactures from less developed countries under the terms of the United Nations Conference on Trade and Development.

The Common Market has also had a long-standing special trade relationship with many of the less developed countries which were former colonies of member countries. The first Yaoundé Convention, operational in 1964, provided for the gradual formation of a free trade area between the Community and 18 less developed countries in Africa. Most imports from these associated states have entered the Community duty-free since July 1, 1968. Products subject to common farm policy controls are considered on a case-by-case basis but associated states are given preference over non-associated states. In return, the associated states have given some preferences to imported goods from the Common Market.

Other less developed countries have negotiated their own arrangements with the Community. In 1966 Nigeria signed an agreement of association which expired without being ratified. Kenya, Uganda and Tanzania signed the Arusha agreement establishing limited reciprocal trade preferences.

New members of the Community must accept the foreign trade policy of the Six original members. Britain will have to align its tariffs on imports from third countries with those of the Community. In the process the average level of tariffs on imports to Britain from third countries will tend to fall from an average 10·2 to 7·6 per cent. Britain will also have to abandon the preferential arrangement negotiated with the Commonwealth countries under the Ottawa Treaty and successive arrangements.

As a result Britain will lose its tariff preferences in Canada, Australia, New Zealand and other Commonwealth countries and they, in turn, will lose their automatic preferences in Britain. The European Free Trade Association agreement will also lapse. Under the terms of the 1971 Brussels negotiations, New Zealand has been secured continuing access to the British market; the Commonwealth sugar producers, except in Australia, have been given certain guarantees for access to the British market; a 'positive attitude' has been promised to the special problems of India, Pakistan and Hong Kong; and 20 other developing countries in the Commonwealth have been offered membership under the Yaoundé pact or a similar form of association.

The Community is also negotiating special arrangements with those members of the European Free Trade Area which do not wish to apply for full membership in the Common Market. The agreement is expected to include free trade in industrial goods, which will effectively preserve an exchange of British goods and those from Sweden, Switzerland and Austria, and vice versa.

Future role of the City of London
The City of London has been the most enthusiastic and wholehearted supporter of British entry to the Common Market, both for political and for economic reasons. The City hopes and expects to become the financial centre of the enlarged Community and to consolidate its unofficial status as the most important financial centre on this side of the Atlantic.

Britain's surplus on private invisible trade (excluding government spending) is much larger than that of any other European country and compares with an actual deficit in Germany. Although less than 20 per cent of Britain's invisible earnings come from Europe at present, in recent years Britain has run consistent surpluses in all sectors of invisible trade with the Continent and especially in financial services including banking insurance and broking of all kinds.

The Committee on Invisible Exports believes that anything which might lead British and overseas people to become more familiar with each other's services and facilities should benefit Britain's invisible account still further and allow the City of London to capitalise on existing advantages. A special study showed that most Common Market policies are still in the formative stage and could be influenced by British attitudes once Britain has joined the Community.

There may be some immediate adverse effect on shipping earnings as a result of the diversion of British trade from long haul routes to the short cross-Channel routes, but this should quickly be recouped by the accelerated growth of total trade which membership is expected to bring. Airline services may also suffer the loss of some long haul air cargo business as the result of diversion of British goods to markets near at hand but the faster growth in passenger traffic and leisure travel is expected to make up for this. Tourism should also benefit in both directions.

Concern has been expressed that British insurance companies may be inhibited by the closer supervision and the restriction of their freedom to invest premium income under standardised Common Market legislation, and this would damage their competitive ability in their more important markets in the U.S. and the Commonwealth. The insurance industry itself believes that standardised legislation is a decade away at least, and that British influence will secure a relatively liberal attitude by the legislators. In the meantime, any greater access to the European market must be beneficial. Banks also believe that anything which allows them to expand their numerous existing business contacts with European companies will be beneficial.

The City already acts as a market for finance for the whole of the developed world outside the United States. The declining importance of sterling as an international currency has made no difference to this market. London is the centre of the Eurodollar market, the pool of internationally-owned currencies outside the control of the national regulations. This market has been a major source of international currency speculation and may be subject to controls and regulations, which could inhibit the market and reduce the City's commissions. But this would occur irrespective of the Common Market membership.

Dollars are expected to remain the principal international currency and the basis unit in which loans are made and accepted by banks and international businesses. In due course, loans could also be denominated in European units of account, but the expertise of London banks would be unimpaired.

The City also hopes to benefit from any possible development of a European stock exchange or federation of stock exchanges, which would encourage international companies to raise equity capital on a community-wide basis. At present, most companies in the Community turn first to their banks or financial institutions for capital rather than to the stock markets. If they were to apply for a quotation on the London Stock Exchange in order to raise equity finance in London, foreign companies would have to disclose much more financial information than is currently in practice to comply with London Stock Exchange regulations. If this reluctance were eliminated, brokers and jobbers could expect much more international business and the financial institutions which invest in international equity issues would also have much more scope in investing funds and in attracting funds from abroad.

7

COMMON MARKET OF THE TEN

Together, the ten members of an enlarged European Community, Britain, Ireland, Norway, Denmark, France, West Germany, Italy, the Netherlands, Belgium and Luxembourg, form the world's largest single market.

Its total population, based on 1969 figures, is 256-million, compared with the United States' 204-million and the Soviet Union's 250-million.

The Ten's combined monetary reserves are more than twice those of the U.S. and more than eight times larger than the U.S.S.R.'s. Total output of motor vehicles and steel in the enlarged Market would exceed that of the U.S. and its combined merchant fleet is more than four times larger than America's.

A ten-power Common Market would be easily the world's largest importer and exporter. Total U.S. production, however, is nearly twice that of the Ten. The Common Market of the Six formed one of the world's major agricultural groups and the second highest meat and milk producer. It was one of the fastest growing of the world's major trading groups.

Community of Ten

The enlargement of the present Community to include Britain, the Irish Republic, Denmark and Norway would greatly increase its economic and political importance. Opposite is how a Market of Ten would compare with the United States, the Soviet Union and Japan. (Figures are for 1969.)

Britain, with a population of 54-million (3·5-million less than West Germany's) leads the Ten in advanced technology, scientific research and development expenditure, coal mining, commercial vehicle production, civil aviation, merchant shipping and agricultural efficiency. It would be the second largest industrial power after West Germany. In view of its size and prestige, the City of London is expected to become the financial centre of the enlarged Market.

West Germany is economically and monetarily much the strongest of the Ten. More than 40 per cent of the industrial production of the Market of the Six comes from the German mines and factories and there seems no reason to suppose that it will not retain its lead

	Six	Ten	U.S.A.	Soviet Union	Japan
Population (millions)	188	256	204	250	102
Gross national production ($ million)	428	564	948	490	167
Sources of gross domestic product—					
Agriculture (%)	6·1	5·8	2·9	—	8·7
Industry (%)	47·5	46·3	36·5	—	39·1
Other activities (%)	46·4	47·9	61·3	—	52·2
Steel production (million metric tons)	109·2	137·0	128·0	110	82·2
Primary energy production (million metric tons coal equivalent)	318·1	506·3	2,020·1	1,050	75·8
Imports ($ million)	39,242[1]	50,000[3]	36,052	—	15,024
Exports ($ million)	39,236[1]	50,000[3]	37,988	—	15,990
Merchant fleet (million tons)[2]	28·1	76·7	18·5	—	27·0
Foreign aid (total capital flow to developing countries $ million)	5,188	6,330	4,645	400	1,263
Monetary reserves[4] ($ million)	21,522	25,676	12,306	—	3,072
Motor vehicles produced (million)	—	10·8	10·1	0·9	4·9

Source: Common Market Commission.

[1] Excluding intra-EEC trade.
[2] July, 1970.
[3] Approximate figures.
[4] October 31, 1970.

in the larger Market. The exceptional drive and enterprise of German industrialists derives partly from the psychological effect of the well-nigh total destruction of large parts of Germany during the Second World War. At the end of 1971 West Germany's total industrial production was about 50 per cent greater than that of France.

Recognising this, President Pompidou has said France's objective is to double its industrial capacity in ten years to achieve an output per head comparable with West Germany's. France would be the third largest industrial power, behind Britain and West Germany, in a Market of Ten, but it has moved into second place in some vital sectors, such as the motor industry. With far more good farmland than any of the nine others, France is the granary of the Market. It was because of German industrial power and France's heavy dependence on agriculture that the Six agreed to create the common agricultural system giving France exceptional benefits. This arises from one of the basic principles of the Common Market: an equitable balance of advantages between member states.

Italy, although fourth on the list, has a population of 52-million, which is not far short of Britain's and West Germany's. Like Britain, its population is increasing more rapidly than West Germany's.

By 1980 it is estimated that Britain, West Germany and Italy will each have a population of about 60-million. Soon after the Market was formed, Italy housed some of the fastest growing industries and has now caught up with France in some industrial sectors.

The Netherlands does well in the Market in electrical engineering, natural gas, chemicals, synthetics, electronics and also gains considerable benefits from the common agricultural policy.

Belgium concentrates on heavy industry and membership of the Market has brought a substantial increase in growth, attracting large-scale investment, notably from the U.S.

Norway leads the Ten in fisheries and, with Britain, in merchant shipping. Denmark, although famous for her agriculture, stands to benefit greatly in the industrial sector of an enlarged Common Market.

Six countries of the Ten are monarchies: Britain, the Netherlands, Belgium, Norway, Denmark and Luxembourg. All ten have democratic, representative systems of government with upper and lower legislative chambers. As members of the Council of Europe, their citizens can bring actions against their own national governments under the Council's Human Rights Convention in safeguarding individual rights. It was under this Convention that Greece, although an associate member of the Common Market, was forced to withdraw from the Council of Europe's Parliamentary Assembly when other member states decided that the Athens military regime denied the basic human freedoms. This decision by the European Human Rights Court was regarded as a valuable precedent for checking any resurgence of extremist nationalism in the larger member states.

All except Ireland are allies in the North Atlantic Treaty Organisation, although France has withdrawn her forces from direct NATO command.

Increased mobility and mass communications have meant that the young in the countries of the Ten have much more in common. Most of the Ten have agreed to put great emphasis on plans for large-scale youth exchanges to break down the old psychological barriers created, not least, by false history textbooks in schools. Since the formation of the Common Market, historians of the Six have been trying to produce accurate histories. Important progress

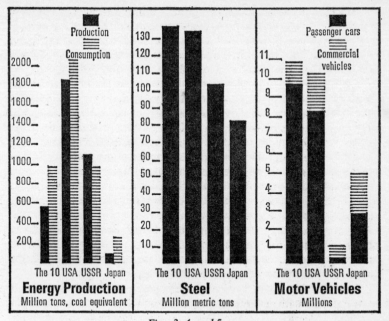

Figs. 3, 4, and 5
Outputs in three important industrial sectors, based on 1969 statistics,
of an enlarged Common Market of ten states and the world's three other
leading producers (*Source:* EEC Commission).

was made on this in the European Schools in Brussels, Luxembourg
and other parts of the Market. Opened at first for the children of
the staffs in the Market's institutions, these schools have grown
rapidly and have won the support of a wider public. There have been
tentative proposals for opening a European School in London. The
schools encourage pupils to approach their studies on a European
rather than a national basis and to spend a very large part of their
time speaking each other's languages.

The biggest political problems in the Community of Ten, apart
from the tensions arising from the Cold War in Eastern Europe and
the Mediterranean, are the division of Germany, the future of
Berlin, the clash between French- and Flemish-speaking Belgians and
the troubles in Northern Ireland. In the field of defence, the central
problem centres on American plans, not clearly formulated in the
early 1970s, to reduce the number of its troops in Western Europe.
There has been general recognition that this could lead eventually
to some form of European defence community, possibly based on an
enlarged Western European Union which was created in 1954 by

Britain and the Six mainly to control West German rearmament. Initiatives have been taken to bring together the Ten negotiating as a group with the U.S. and the Soviet Union in a European Security Conference, although the U.S.S.R. has refused to recognise the European Communities and has sharply opposed British entry.

There are hopes that British entry into the Common Market will speed up plans to build a Channel Tunnel by the end of the decade if only because of the expected increase in the volume of goods flowing between Britain and the Continent. Flying time from London to the capitals of the other nine countries ranges from under an hour (Paris and Brussels) to two hours (Rome and Oslo). A businessman or anyone else with important appointments to keep should note that air services are frequently halted by fog in winter and to a considerable extent in the rest of the year. Telephone services between the Ten have been improved but are still so limited that there are long periods during which Britain is cut off from many of them. Cost of an ordinary meal in Market capitals ranges from just over a pound (Amsterdam) to well beyond two pounds for a relatively moderate meal in Paris or Brussels.

The following chapters describe each of the ten countries that have agreed to form the enlarged Common Market. Each country also has a Statistics Sheet located at the end of the text, pp. 173–8.

8

BRITAIN

To the late Dean Acheson, former U.S. Secretary of State, Britain was a nation that had lost an empire and was consequently in search of a new role. The quest is all-embracing, one that is economic and industrial, as well as social and political.

Possessing a ready-made trading bloc in the Commonwealth, the historical product of a comfortable imperial market for industry to exploit and develop, Britain built tariff walls behind which it could shelter. But the Commonwealth markets have lacked the growth of Europe and the U.S., a fact which, coupled with Britain's slow expansion, has added to the urgency of the need for change in the trading base. Commonwealth countries accounted for more than 37 per cent of Britain's exports when the Common Market was born. The proportion was down to 21 per cent in 1970 when the Common Market's share had jumped from 14 to 22 per cent and the stop-gap EFTA, with half-hearted British support, accounted for 16 per cent against ten per cent.

The United States has become the largest single market (whisky is the money spinner), followed by Germany and Ireland. The Commonwealth countries have turned to Japan and the U.S. These changing relationships have propelled Britain increasingly faster towards another industrial revolution.

Its first, producing the massive transfer of people from land to factory that still bedevils Common Market policy, laid the basis for its industrial prosperity. This second has involved overhauling existing machinery, in need of a regeneration through new markets.

However, Britain is still one of the world's five major trading nations, although losing ground quickly. Trade and manufacture represent its lifeline, for its natural resources are limited to coal, timber and, more recently, a bonus in the form of offshore gas and oil. It has lived by its inventiveness, initiative, industry and phlegmatic character that produce envy and frustration from both admirers and critics.

Increasingly, though, Britain's share in world markets has been eroded as it has been overtaken by more efficient and modern industrial machines, notably the U.S., West Germany and Japan. A recurring balance of payments crisis has produced cause for anxiety. An agonising introspection together with a peculiar insularity, despite the Commonwealth, have proved bewildering to the rest of the world. Britain's share of international trade in manufactured goods has dropped from an eighth to a tenth in recent years; this has been countered by devaluation, prices and incomes control, and several attempts to reflate and deflate, all administered with mixed degrees of success. The rate of economic growth has lagged seriously behind its major competitors (Britain's growth between 1958-69 was on average about three per cent, compared to the Common Market's 5·5 per cent). Other yardsticks yield equally disturbing results: productivity and capital investment (Britain's investment as a proportion of GNP has been 17 per cent, compared to the Common Market's 21 per cent where the need for new plant and machinery has of course been pressing).

Historically, Britain has been regarded as the 'workshop of the world'. Its manufacturing base was widely spread and its product range, quality and reliability unchallenged. The manufacturing industry, with engineering the cornerstone, still accounts for about a third of production; agriculture, mining, forestry and fishing account for another five per cent, and building and construction about 12 per cent. Its farmers still provide about half the nation's food, compared to the third before the Second World War with a smaller labour force. (For every agricultural worker there are about 13 working in manufacturing industry.)

The industrial base shows the scars of time. The 1960s featured accelerated changes in its traditional backbone: the rundown of coal mining, the decline of the shipbuilding industry and the steel industry that has earned the unenviable description of a 'working museum'; cotton textiles have been almost strangled by competition from low-cost imports from Commonwealth countries with cheap labour bases.

The fundamental change in emphasis produced by the challenge of technology has spawned more sophisticated and demanding (on money and resources) industries such as electronics, computers, aerospace, man-made fibres, and accelerated the process and need for change. It has tapped new reservoirs of skill and inventiveness, but Britain has no monopoly on either and the absence of a large domestic market place on which to capitalise has inhibited progress. The enormous investment demanded by technology, coupled with the need for a larger market (British industry does not have the benefits of the sizable military contracts that support American technical efforts), has strengthened the case for joint ventures with other countries and the sharing of the financial load. The expenditure in nuclear power, for example, while gaining a world-lead, has yet to produce economic dividends.

There also remains the basic imbalance between the prosperous south and the sizable northern pockets of depression. London and the Southeast, with about a third of the population, is still largely a service area, the seat of economic, political and social power; the Midlands continues as the heart of the engineering and motor industries; Yorkshire and Lancashire provide coal and steel resources, wool and cotton textiles. Then there are the industries of South Wales and the Northeast, and the engineering and shipbuilding centres of Scotland's Clydeside and Northern Ireland.

Government, management and labour have all failed to come to terms with fundamental structural changes in industry resulting in tortuous labour disputes and the disruption and anguish left by strikes, which in such major disputes as those on the docks and in the motor car factories contributed so much to the economic crises of the 1960s. Whether the three interested parties can achieve a consensus, through which to work, under the 1971 Industrial Relations Act remains to be seen. The legacy left by poverty, wages and high unemployment has widened the gap between management and labour. Economic survival is dependent on erasing the resulting bitter memories.

The size of industry has changed significantly, as has the emphasis, leading to a creating of larger units in the late 1960s, particularly in electrical engineering, motor cars and computers, to compete more effectively with bigger American companies. Extensive rationalisation has also created larger units in textiles, shipbuilding and brewing. Steel has been the major addition to the vast public sector. On the other hand, the small businessman continues an increasingly difficult struggle to avoid folding or merging. An estimated 1·75-million of a total working population of 25-million are in business for themselves either individually or employing small numbers.

Size has also dominated the debate on the future of local government with proposals to transform the conurbations of Birmingham, Manchester, Liverpool and Glasgow into self-governing units (four out of five people live in towns) and to bite into green acres that still separate town from country.

Britain has also shed quickly its label as a cheap labour country, formerly an attraction for foreign investors, and narrowed the gap with its Common Market counterparts. Average British earnings increased by less than 40 per cent in real terms between 1958 and 1969 compared with the Community average of more than 75 per cent. But the inflationary spiral of 1969–70 has resulted in a sharp increase in earnings of about 13 per cent in 1970 and in prices of eight per cent, double the historical average. Inflation is not a British prerogative but the absence of any parallel rise in productivity, that has accompanied inflation in the Common Market countries, has added to the pressures on competitiveness.

More dramatically, perhaps, the structures and attitudes of society have undergone more change in post-War years than the Victorians and Edwardians managed together. The emergence of a 'propertied' middle-class democracy (complete with mortgages and commuting), the resurrection of Celtic nationalism, the undermining of the welfare state dream have all combined to force the old order to change. The extension of the education system has hastened a change in the staffing of government, industry and business administration, a change which has brought new ethics and practices. The remaining institutions have necessarily lagged and the lines of delineation have been blurred as new interest groups penetrate these institutions. This is manifested best in the ever-changing stances adopted by the political parties, each of which attempts to straddle the middle and establish itself as the party of consensus: the Conservatives attempt to present a more middle-class image endeavouring to shed their big business trappings; Labour has 'traded upwards' from its working-class roots; the Liberals have become a resort for traditionalists and disenchanted youth.

The consumer society, born out of 'never had it so good' and nurtured by never-never land, has generated new attitudes and the English language has echoed with new catch phrases such as the 'white-hot technological revolution' and, more latterly, 'lame duck'. Five families out of six have television sets, two in three washing machines, one in two refrigerators. More than half of all houses and flats are owner-occupied. The motor car population has more than doubled, to over 12-million, in the past ten years, the car simultaneously declining as a status symbol; one in five families now go in search of foreign sunshine for their holidays. The pattern of spending has shifted: food has fallen (but not calorie intake) as a percentage of spending, as the cost of housing and transport has risen.

Of every £ earned, about 34p goes in taxation and national insurance (about 14p on direct taxes), another 7p in national savings, 15p on food, 9p on housing, 6p on clothing, 5p on consumer durables (washing machines, televisions, refrigerators and the like), 5p on drink, 4p on motor vehicles and 4p on tobacco.

Beneath the commercial veneer the pressure and pace of life have increased, disturbing the traditional British calm and creating in its wake a variety of lobbies and pressure groups. Unemployment has not lost its stigma despite an intricate system of supplementary payments, technology and machines have shed some of their glamour, although still causing apprehension. The permissive society has uncorked a new brand of liberalism that questions the traditional values and perplexes the young as well as the old. Race has become an issue since the influx of coloured immigrants has increased the size of work force at a time when there has been no corresponding increase in the number of available jobs.

Finally, the belated discovery that the environment is being threatened by industry and the urban sprawl has produced alarm concerning a deterioration in the quality of life. But Britain has a reputation for tolerance and pragmatism, perhaps best evidenced as the basis for the support it could continually call upon in Europe as it strove to gain entry into the Common Market.

CHANNEL ISLANDS AND THE ISLE OF MAN

The Six agreed with Mr. Rippon in November 1971 to offer the Channel Islands and the Isle of Man a special arrangement to meet difficulties which could arise in the islands as a result of British entry into the Market.

The main points of the arrangement are:

> For industrial products the main external tariff of the Market (CET) will be applied to the islands. Within this there would be free movement of goods between them and all Market member states.
>
> For agricultural products the Market's system of applying levies on food imports from non-member countries would apply in the islands together with certain other parts of the common agricultural policy (CAP) required to maintain free trade in farm produce.
>
> Other provisions of the Rome Treaty will apply to the extent necessary for introducing and operating these arrangements.
>
> A non-discrimination clause will preserve the islanders' rights in Britain; but there will be no discrimination between the treatment of British visitors to, or residents in, the islands and nationals of other Market countries.

If difficulties arise over the agreements the island authorities could discuss the removal of these difficulties as an alternative to application of safeguards.

9

REPUBLIC OF IRELAND

Economically, Ireland is heavily dependent on Britain. More than half its imports in 1970 originated in Britain (53·5 per cent or £354-million) while 65 per cent of its exports, valued at £287-million, made the short journey across the Irish Sea.

The trade balance has traditionally been strongly in Britain's favour. But the 'flu syndrome, Ireland catches a cold when Britain sneezes, has played a significant part in restricting growth and influencing policy (rising unemployment in Britain also means fewer jobs for Irish construction workers and less cash remitted to dependants).

The Anglo-Irish trade agreement, involving a gradual dismantling of tariff barriers by 1975, has strengthened the economic dependence, historically uncomfortable though it may be. In many guises it represents a trial run for Ireland before the Common Market becomes reality.

The fear that its agriculturally-based economy would not be able to withstand the competitive market created by free trade has dominated economic thinking and sustained a protectionist outlook. Removal of the high tariff walls could cost up to ten-thousand jobs according to some early estimates and the experience provided by the trade agreement has been revealing. British exports to Ireland have jumped sharply, from £178·5-million in 1967, while trade in the other direction, principally beef and dairy products, has developed more slowly from a corresponding level of £169-million.

Sections of the textile trade have shown signs of labouring under the effects of competition well before all the tariffs are removed and there is the inevitable concern that more damage will be caused by Market entry.

The Irish economy is vulnerable. The purchase of a Jumbo jet by its state airline (£25-million including spares) would be sufficient to produce major balance of payments headaches. The trading deficit in 1970 was £207-million (£62-million in balance of payments terms).

Ireland has generally followed Britain along the road to Brussels, throughout the abortive series of negotiations during the 1960s, for much the same reasons: the need for access to greater markets and, more particularly, because it cannot stand alone.

The Common Market holds out prospects of lessening dependence on Britain and widening the trading base, however, the economic tie is unlikely to be significantly loosened. The terms negotiated at Brussels protect the free trade agreement and important agricultural links during the transitional period.

Overall, Ireland has emerged with roughly the same arrangements as Britain for the tariff breakdown during the changeover; but, while Britain is looking for industrial gains, Ireland is predictably banking on agriculture to produce its dividends.

The constitutional change posed by Common Market entry involves a referendum, likely towards the end of 1972. A simple majority will be sufficient to approve application irrespective of the size of vote and, while the loss of sovereignty and fisheries safeguards have been raised as issues, the prospect of entry into the Common Market has generated relatively little interest.

Irish exporters' prospects

The benefits for Irish exporters could be significant. Producers of cattle and beef, milk and dairy products, and sheep and lambs are in for a major breakthrough. And the Government White Paper claims higher feed bills facing pig and poultry producers could be met by more efficiency.

It is estimated that application of the common agricultural policy (CAP) could increase farm income overall by a net £100-million, or 55 per cent above current levels. However, while farming efficiency has been increasing slowly, the structure of the industry reflects many of the Community's agricultural problems. The average sized farm holding is about 40 acres and the vast majority of Ireland's 260-thousand farms are in the 15–100 acre category.

Horticulture, as in Britain, would suffer in the face of competition from existing Common Market producers.

About four-fifths of agricultural output is livestock and associated products and the farm industry estimates that application of CAP could mean a 60 per cent rise in beef prices, up to 70 per cent in milk and 25 per cent for pigs and barley (a substantial part of it coming from Britain), producing in its wake a fresh round of expansion for beef production and providing a further check to the fall in the sheep population.

Gross agricultural output by the end of the decade could be running 30–40 per cent above present levels while domestic food prices could be 11–16 per cent higher and the cost-of-living 3–4·5 per cent during the transitional period. Contribution to the CAP at the end of the period is expected to work out at about £9·7-million, the flow in the other direction will be much greater and, in addition, there will be a £36-million saving in support subsidies.

Ireland has gained concessions on two important domestic issues. They are dumping and extended protection for its small, struggling motor industry which could disintegrate rapidly under the strain of open competition. The government will still be able to exercise its own rather than Community anti-dumping rules and retain what it regards as a more effective umbrella over its small manufacturing base. This dispensation will only cover the transitional period.

Ireland originally wanted protection in two sensitive industries: jute and cars. The jute industry, as one government official commented laconically, solved its own problems by folding. Protection for the motor industry will extend over a 12-year period and involves continued limitations on imports to allow its already heavily-taxed domestic assembly industry to develop almost unmolested. Cars in Ireland run at little more than one-to-eight per capita, offering access for Continental mass producers, while the cost of providing three-thousand domestic jobs has been an expensive subsidy.

The government believes Ireland will net gain substantially from foreign investment and, while there are likely to be changes in its sizable incentives, tax harvests and the like to meet Community criteria, there are sufficient indications to suggest that its industrialisation programme will continue largely unimpeded and that, like southern Italy, it will benefit from dispensations. The Community has agreed that the whole of the Irish Republic should be regarded as a development region.

Ireland has already gained significantly from inward investment following the intensive drive to attract industry although about 40 per cent of the projects involved have originated from Britain. Ireland's existing export tax relief arrangements are safeguarded after entry. There are many natural attractions, deep-water facilities for supertankers, space and surplus labour, despite a limited market. The Commission has the right to review export incentives. The EEC will put additional pressure on location policy: attracting industry from the east coast, closest to European markets, to the picturesque Atlantic coast (development of the Shannon industrial estate, with its attraction of total tax exemption until 1983, represents the most imaginative move in the west).

Additionally, there will be more markets eager to take up Irish labour, although the language barrier is expected to act in favour of Britain's construction industry.

Ireland is looking, as is Britain, for a 'dynamic' impetus from the Market. Its growth rate has slowed from a record 7·9 per cent in 1968 to 4 per cent in 1969 and 1·5 per cent in 1970. Its industrial base is still relatively undeveloped, needs more nourishment and has been geared mainly to meet the needs of the home rather than export market (about 70 per cent of manufacturing output is designed for domestic consumption). Guinness still represents a sizable export along with clothing but, while the number of companies producing electrical machinery is growing, the contrast with the more heavily industrialised and equally heavily subsidised manufacturing base in the north is still significant.

Industry allied with tourism has none the less accounted for much of the growth and the Common Market boost for agriculture will produce a spin-off for manufacturing companies.

The absence of a skilled pool of workers, blamed on deficiencies in education and training (and emigration), is however inhibiting development and Ireland's industrial relations record, as well as its failure until recently to introduce more effective prices and incomes control, has been as bad as Britain's.

The trade umbrella provided by Britain will continue to ensure an element of competition against new Common Market competitors and there is some hope that, indirectly, the EEC will make some contribution in ultimately uniting the six northern counties to the 26 southern.

10

FRANCE

France provides the fulcrum for the European Community and has so far exercised the strongest influence on its political development. Its economic and political leaders invented the Common Market, launched it, led it and came very near to destroying it.

After being designed by Jean Monnet and Robert Schuman as a federation, President de Gaulle remoulded it into a *Europe des patries*, in which each member state held on to the right of veto. Yet the industry of some of France's top civil servants has contributed much to the effectiveness of the Brussels institutions.

The Franco-German Treaty of Friendship signed in Paris in 1963 by de Gaulle and Chancellor Adenauer in many ways contradicted the basic principles of the Community. But without Franco-German reconciliation there could not have been a Community.

Again, it was President Pompidou's historic gesture of friendship to Britain at his meeting with Prime Minister Heath in 1971 that opened the way for British entry and the unity of almost the whole of Western Europe. The new entente, for which Christopher Soames, British Ambassador to Paris, can claim much credit, came while West Germany was defying France in the dispute over monetary policy in Brussels and was thought by the French to be running grave risks with her *Ostpolitik* (see Chapter 11).

The extreme political instability of post-War France, culminating in the Algerian war, disappeared with the creation of the Fifth Republic and General de Gaulle's return to power in 1958. The next ten years were marked by de Gaulle's policy of granting independence to France's former colonies and carrying out a rapprochement with Eastern Europe, while steering an independent course between the two world power blocs.

At home, political stability began increasingly to be accompanied by social and industrial unrest. In May, 1968, the student and workers' strike came close to defeating the government. A strong 'law-and-order' backlash returned the Gaullists to power in June with a large majority in the legislature; but de Gaulle retired the following year after being defeated by a national referendum on regional reform measures. His successor, Georges Pompidou, has continued most of his policies, including that of retaining the power of the presidency.

French economic policy has aimed, with considerable success, at combining a high rate of expansion with monetary stability. Inflation, the world monetary crisis and growing pressure for increased wages have been met with firm policies. Their long-term success may well be confirmed or denied by international difficulties affecting all countries.

Trade with Britain

British exports and re-exports to France in 1970 totalled £339·23-million in value. From January to June, 1971, they were £157·43-million, representing an increase of about 12·2 per cent in value. In view of an increase in export prices of about ten per cent, the increase in volume of British exports to France can be estimated at about three per cent. This is considered a normal upward trend reflecting the growth of our exports over the last few years. Exports alone, not including classic re-exports (tea, raw materials, re-processed products, etc.), are running at about £325-million a year. Within this total, about 50 per cent is represented by capital goods, mostly machinery. The remainder comprises consumer goods, limited raw materials and other items, including food and beverages (mainly Scotch whisky).

Britain imports beef from France, a process enhanced by British preference for the forequarters of the animal and French preference for the hindquarters, which leads to a natural exchange.

Similarly, since lamb and mutton are prized delicacies on the French market, there is an important export of sheepmeat from Britain to France: under existing Common Market regulations sheepmeat can be imported by France if prices on the French market rise above a certain level on three consecutive Mondays. Fresh and chilled meat are shipped in vans (no frozen meat is allowed). This trade totals about £5-million a year.

British exporters' prospects　The bulk of British exports to France is in the machinery sector. France is still relatively underindustrialised: though a highly organised country at an earlier date than Britain, the circumstances of French history did not lead to the rapid industrialisation experienced by Britain and Germany. Now France is gaining, with the advantage that many industrial developments are being launched for the first time without the need to change from old and established patterns. For some time, France will still need to import the specialised, sophisticated equipment for complete modern industrialisation.

This industrial sector is likely to provide the continuing element of growth in British exports, especially since the underlying aim of

French economic planning is accelerated industrialisation. British industrial exports are expected to continue to expand at a gradually accelerating rate. This is not so much because of the removal of tariff barriers but because Britain's inclusion in the Common Market is expected to stimulate British manufacturers to pay more attention to Continental Europe.

Another element likely to promote increased British participation in French (and other European) growth is the Common Market's rule of Community preference. This establishes guidelines which encourage firms, especially those susceptible to government influence (i.e. most French firms), to seek to supply their needs first in France, then among the Six and only at third choice, in non-member countries. Community members, including Britain, will therefore have an advantage.

However, the main impact on British exports of entry into the Market is likely to be on consumer goods, at present somewhat held in check by the Common Market tariff and various non-tariff barriers. Consumer goods are, by nature, much more susceptible to competitive prices and in 1971 British consumer goods paid a 10–11 per cent ad valorem tariff, *plus* VAT (value-added tax). This tax will remain, but the progressive removal of the import tariff, together with the abolition of some remaining quotas and other impediments, is likely to be highly advantageous. Present quotas apply to frozen fish, jam, marmalade, some electronic components and pleasure boats (up to a certain size). Some British firms have already established French manufacturing subsidiaries and are selling jams and marmalades in France at marketable prices. There is a substantial luxury trade in British foodstuffs. The prospects for introducing British tinned goods, biscuits and many other lines into the mass retail market (supermarkets, co-operatives, etc.) will undoubtedly improve as the tariffs are reduced and finally removed.

The general recommendations made to British exporters in the post-War years on increased competition apply particularly in the sophisticated French market. Business is normally conducted in French and, although a growing number of French executives speak English, a knowledge of French is essential to British salesmen and visiting executives. All sales literature should be in French and firms should, where possible, send plenipotentiary sales representatives who are empowered to conclude terms. Business is likely to be lost while junior salesmen return to Britain to consult their superiors. On these and other sales promotion points, the annual booklet 'Hints to Business Men' (France), published by the Export Services Division of Department of Trade and Industry, is useful.

French opinion of British exports is generally high. The usual complaints are made about delivery dates and after-sales service. While such criticism applies to all exporting countries and failures receive much more publicity than successes, it is obviously desirable for British firms to keep on their toes and provide efficient and courteous service in the old tradition, while adapting to modern competitive standards. This is the advice given by the British Chamber of Commerce in Paris.

French exporters' prospects in Britain   France is not a traditionally export-minded country. Of its one-million major manufacturing concerns five-hundred alone account for 80–85 per cent of total sales abroad and about a dozen of these firms are responsible for 50–60 per cent of the exports.

The evolution of the French export (and import) market since the last War has shown a relative decline in trade with Britain and a heavy increase in trade with the Common Market countries, particularly West Germany. It is interesting, too, that among the EFTA countries, Switzerland (population about six-million) imports more from France than does Britain (population over 55-million).

France's average *monthly* exports in 1970 were £623-million of which Britain took £25-million. West Germany, France's largest single customer, took £128-million and Italy £69·4-million. Exports to Switzerland averaged £29·4-million.

The prospect of the imminent entry of Britain into the Common Market has already provoked a renewal of interest among French exporters and a flood of inquiries is now received daily at the Comité National du Commerce Extérieur, a quasi-autonomous body which provides market surveys and other services to exporters. As in the British case, it is in consumer goods, particularly dairy products such as cheeses, other foods and beverages that the main expansion is expected to occur.

The 1969 pattern of principal French exports was as follows:

Capital goods	24	per cent of total exports	
Consumer goods	24	,,	,,	,,
Semi-manufactures	22	,,	,,	,,
Food products	18	,,	,,	,,
Raw materials	8	,,	,,	,,
Other	4	,,	,,	,,
	100	per cent		

Source: French customs returns.

Trade with the Irish Republic

The Irish Republic's membership in the Common Market is expected to lead to higher returns for exports of Irish foodstuffs such as beef, lamb and pigmeat.

Irish exports to France in 1970 were approximately £13·5-million and imports from France about £21-million. The bulk of Irish exports consisted of meat and other agricultural products including about £2-million of lamb, £900-thousand of horsemeat (a popular food for children in France) and £300-thousand of pork. Ores and concentrates accounted for nearly £4-million and there is a growing trade in surgical instruments and appliances (about £2·5-million in 1970).

In general, Ireland is hoping for a diversification of exports and a lessening dependence on the British market, especially in the field of agriculture. Longer term prospects for industrial development within the Common Market's regional development policies, when these are worked out, are also considered to be favourable.

11

WEST GERMANY

The political scene in West Germany has been dominated since Willy Brandt became Chancellor in 1969, as the head of the country's first Social Democratic government, by *Ostpolitik* (or 'normalising' relations with the Soviet Union and the East European Communist countries). Treaties have been signed with Moscow and Warsaw but these await parliamentary ratification until a satisfactory agreement can be reached on the Berlin issue. After 18 months of negotiations, the outline of such an agreement was signed by the ambassadors of the four post-War occupying powers in September, 1971; but details remained to be filled in by East–West German negotiations. These ran into unexpected translation difficulties so that, by mid-September, no start had been made on the chief difficulty, concerned mainly with the Berlin access routes. The ambassadors had agreed that travel to and from isolated West Berlin should be made easier but left details to the Germans.

On the economic side, West Germany, long known as the country of the post-War 'miracle' recovery, continues on its path of what seems at least in the eyes of the outside world permanent prosperity. There was a minor recession in 1966–7, but the aim of maintaining full employment and a stable currency has been achieved more successfully than in most western countries. The mark remains (together with the Swiss franc), and particularly since the dollar ran into trouble, one of the two hardest currencies in the world. None of this means that no fears need be entertained about the economic future of West Germany. There were difficulties in the early 1970s such as the steeply-falling profits of Volkswagen, the country's biggest commercial undertaking, and the closing down of the country's oldest camera firm in face of Japanese competition. Unemployment was at a mere 150-thousand or so, negligible compared with Britain's, which has a labour force of similar size; but it threatens in a number of sectors of industry including coal, steel and office machinery. The average rate of growth of West Germany's GNP (gross national product) during the first ten years of the Common Market was at 6·6 per cent. This was below that of Italy (8·8), the Netherlands (8·2), France (7·8), and above Belgium (6·3) and Luxembourg (5·1); though well above Britain's with barely 2·5 per cent. By the 1970s, while the rate was declining in both Italy and France, it was being maintained and even slightly increased in West Germany at about seven per cent. Since 1952 West Germany has had a favourable balance of trade and, in spite of successive revaluations including floating rates for the mark, continued to maintain and even increase it. In August, 1971, it was about £1,200-million compared with £1,150-million in the same period of 1970.

Coal output was falling but planned output for 1971 was still 110-million tons. This meant that coal had at last been replaced as a source of primary power (43·1 per cent) by oil (49·6 per cent). Imports of oil rose by several million tons annually (89·5-million tons in 1970). Increasing quantities of natural gas (8·75-million cubic yards in 1970) were also being used. These supplies came from home resources but more was being obtained from the Netherlands and more still was soon due from the U.S.S.R. Estimated requirements for 1980 were 60-million cubic yards.

Steel production in West Germany last year was 43·8-million tons. This made it the major producer (45·3 per cent) in the European Coal and Steel Community. Production in Britain was 26·9-million tons.

Motor vehicle production in West Germany in 1970 was 3,107,000 units, compared with 2,198,488 in Britain. Shipping output was 1,237-thousand tons, compared with Britain's 1,798-thousand tons. The value of the output of the electrical industry in 1969 was £4,841-million, of which about one-third consisted of consumer goods such as radio and television sets, household appliances, including washing machines, refrigerators, mixers, etc. France is the largest supplier (13 per cent) of West Germany's imports.

The general political state of the country since Konrad Adenauer formed his first government in 1949 has been one of remarkable stability. This has been in part a consequence of the determination of Chancellor Adenauer and his right-wing Christian Democratic successors, Ludwig Erhard and Kurt Kiesinger) to place and maintain their country's footing in the western alliance. This policy has been followed by Chancellor Brandt and his Foreign Minister, Walter Scheel, in spite of the attempt to achieve 'an opening to the East'.

This stability has also been due in part to the West German system which has avoided the mistakes of its Weimar predecessor. The president (Gustav Heinemann) has no political power and the chancellor, the chief political figure, cannot be dismissed from office by the Bundestag except by a vote which simultaneously appoints his successor. The difficulties posed by this operation have enabled a number of governments, including Brandt's, to remain in power with very narrow majorities.

Trade with Britain
British exporters supply four per cent of West Germany's imports, which means that Britain is sixth on the list of suppliers. After remaining for some time in favour of West Germany, Anglo-German trade was roughly in balance in 1970 (nearly £550-million each). But in 1971 there was, in the first half of the year, a trend favouring West Germany. While German exports to Britain were rising at the rate of about 19 per cent, British exports to West Germany were rising at about five or six per cent.

West German industrialists have always backed Britain's application for entry to the Common Market because of the prospect of increased trade in both directions. Trade between West Germany and Britain is mainly in the field of capital goods, with machinery heading the list both ways. Chemicals also come high in both directions, though non-ferrous metals were second for Britain in 1970.

British exporters' prospects Prospects for Britain, when the trade barriers fall, appear to be best in the field of machinery, though the outlook for motor vehicles (especially trucks) and textiles and carpets is thought to be good. On the whole, German industrialists think highly of British goods. though there are some exceptions concerned with quality and after-sales service, including supply of spares. As an example, one Cologne agent for British machine tools speaks enthusiastically of one British firm but thinks so little of another that he has given up on the agency.

No sudden transformation of trade is expected as the roughly ten per cent duties will fall gradually during the transitional period. If British exporters are to realise, after Britain's entry, the full potential of the West German market they will have to be aware of a number of German susceptible areas. These include a preference for quotations in their own language and in the metric system. If new to the market, British exporters would do well to consult in advance the Department of Trade and Industry or the commercial section of the British Embassy in Bonn or a British consulate which can be found in any major town. Exporters wishing to operate inside Germany, as distinct from selling direct to a German buyer, would do well to appoint a German agent (or several, if they wish to cover the entire country); or to establish a private limited company (G.m.b.H.). Turnover equalisation tax is levied on most goods imported into West Germany at a rate of 11 per cent and five and a half per cent for the rest (mostly agricultural).

German exporters' prospects in Britain Following Britain's entry, Germans generally see their best prospects to be in their traditional fields of machinery (both electric and non-electric), chemicals, transport equipment and cars.

West Germany's chief exports, in order, are: non-electrical machinery, motor vehicles, chemicals, electrical machinery, iron and steel, textiles and yarn fabrics, precision instruments, optical and photo-chemical products, coal, coke and briquettes. Following France as West Germany's biggest export market are the Netherlands, the U.S., Belgium (including Luxembourg), Italy, Switzerland and Austria; all precede Britain.

Trade with the Irish Republic

The best prospects for Irish exporters, if Ireland joins the Market with Britain and the other applicants, appear to be mainly in the field of meat, including mutton, in which exports have fallen from £5-million a year to zero under the Common Market's agricultural policy. Ireland at present exports copper and some manufactures to West Germany, but to a total only of about £12-million, compared with £40- to £50-million received in return. Even after entry into the Common Market, there is little prospect of achieving a balance.

12

ITALY

At a quick glance, maps of the old Roman Empire, apart from the barbarian-occupied northeastern areas, look very much like a map of the Common Market. The Italians, proud heirs of two-thousand years of Roman and Renaissance civilisation, frequently remind their Market partners in long, often passionate, pronouncements in Brussels that the European idea is as old as Rome and that the Romans laid the foundations for the lasting European union of Christendom.

Despite their eagerness for total European unity, it is only a century since the Italians managed to unite their own nation. They have maintained their unity and stability with difficulty because of the enormous gap between the rich north and the poor south.

By importing raw materials from its partners and exporting them back as highly competitive cars, refrigerators and other manufactured goods, Italy has done well in the Common Market. Its growth has increased by nearly four-hundred per cent since the 1950s. In contrast, despite large-scale development plans, southern Italy remains an acute problem. Well over one and a half million people are estimated to have left the Mezzogiorno between 1951 and 1962. This has reduced its chances of achieving satisfactory growth. It is not surprising therefore that Italy has the largest Communist party in the West (a quarter of the electorate). Its leaders, defying Moscow, have come out in favour of the Market and British entry. Labour unrest has cost Italy millions of pounds in strikes in the last two years.

Fiat, Italy's largest car manufacturer, has reported a heavy decline in production. Pirelli, the privately-owned tyre and rubber company, has asked workers at Milan to retire before the normal retirement age, offering tempting compensation payments. The company said it intended closing non-productive sections.

Emilio Colombo, head of the centre-left coalition government, has managed to maintain some stability, although under criticism for tardiness in meeting Italy's needs for reform. Communist pressure for posts in the government has been prevented by strong opposition from Colombo's own Christian Democrats, backed by the Vatican.

Trade with Britain

In the second half of 1971, Britain's exports to Italy showed a slow but consistent increase. The main British exports to Italy during the early part of 1971 were hides, textile fibres, crude fertilisers and minerals, metalliferous ores, chemicals, leather manufactures, paper and paper board manufactures, textile yarn and fabrics, non-metallic mineral manufactures, iron and steel, non-ferrous metals, metal manufactures, machinery, transport equipment, scientific, optical and photographic goods, and beverages.

Under beverages, Scotch and Irish whisky are increasingly popular. Scotch and Irish whisky exporters began a drive to expand sales to Italy two years ago. The Italians, traditionally wine and beer drinkers, have shown signs of following the American way of drinking. There has been a marked swing to spirits, with whisky topping the list. Italian selling prices are quite reasonable, varying from £2·40 a bottle to £5·12 for special blends. The Health Ministry recently drew attention to the 'increasing consumption of high alcoholic content liquor'.

Italy's imports from Common Market countries include cattle, pigs, scrap iron and copper, frozen meat, butter, cheese, tobacco, textiles, rolled iron and steel, industrial machinery (high on the list), aluminium, chemicals, synthetic fibres, electric light bulbs and rubber products including motor tyres.

Italian exports to Market partners have been mainly: fresh fruit and vegetables, canned foods, cut flowers, wines, synthetic fibre products, wool and synthetic fibre materials, shoes and leather goods, cars, refrigerators, typewriters and industrial equipment.

Italy is also developing trade with the United States, the Scandinavian and East European countries, the Soviet Union (which has a large Fiat car factory), Japan, China and in the Middle East.

British exporters' prospects Official and private business observers say there is a 'very good' chance that Britain can substantially increase its trade after entry into the Common Market.

Italian importers of British goods believe British chemicals, textiles and yarn-fabrics, non-ferrous metals, iron and steel, machinery and transport equipment should show rapid increases as the tariffs come down. There should also be expansion in other products and traders are investigating the prospects for widening the range of British exports.

Italian businessmen often praise British business and organisational methods as being among the best in the world. They suggest that, although many of them have a working knowledge of English or employ secretary-translators, letters from British firms should be in Italian. Misunderstandings over English technical terms could lead to loss of orders.

British businessmen visiting Italy should, it is suggested, have a fair working knowledge of Italian so that interpreters and translators are not needed.

Italian exporters' prospects in Britain   Italian firms place emphasis on the expectations for electric domestic appliances, textiles, shoes, wines, fruit and a wide range of canned foods.

13

THE NETHERLANDS

For all sorts of reasons, the Netherlands can be regarded as Britain's gateway to Europe. Amsterdam is less than an hour's flight from London; a British businessman can get to the Netherlands in less time than from London to Manchester. When he touches down, he finds that most educated Dutchmen speak fluent English. In no other Common Market country does he feel so much at home in so short a time. The Dutch have a deep-rooted affinity with the British dating back over centuries of shared maritime and mercantile traditions. It is little wonder that many British regard the Dutch as their best friends on the Continent, nor is it an accident that the Netherlands led by its Foreign Minister, Joseph Luns, has always championed British entry into the Common Market.

Without Rotterdam at the mouth of the Rhine, conveyor-belt to the industrial heart of Europe, the Netherlands would perhaps be little more than the tourist image of a nation comprising tulips, windmills and wooden shoes. But Rotterdam, the world's busiest port, has enabled the country to become a channel for an enormous share of the Common Market's exports and imports. Rotterdam and Amsterdam each boast just over a million inhabitants in a land of 13-million people; but, as port and centre of industrial development, Rotterdam is far ahead of the capital city.

Politically, the Netherlands is more stable than its multiplicity of political parties might suggest. After each election, there is a prolonged political 'crisis' while the various Catholic, Protestant, Liberal, Labour and several fringe parties and splinter groups, bargain over the formation of a new ruling coalition. These seldom cause major disturbances in the maintenance of the economic and social status quo.

The Netherlands' industrial revolution has reduced its (highly competitive) agriculture to the point at which it employs only seven per cent of the national work force. Much of the recent expansion has been in the modern growth industries, notably chemicals and electronics. Until the end of 1963, wages were kept low by common agreement, but then the economic dykes burst: during the last eight years, wages have increased at a rate of more than ten per cent annually. By 1969 the average hourly wage of an industrial worker was more than seven guilders (about 80 pence) an hour, and in the following two years it rose by a further 25 per cent. The unions are still demanding and gaining wage rises at the rate of 12·5 per cent annually, maintaining an inflation rate which is the highest in the Common Market. These figures include employer contributions to social services which are generally similar in scope and coverage to those in most countries of the Six, and rather better than the system in Belgium. Although taxes have been rising faster in the Netherlands than elsewhere in the Market, the average burden of tax per citizen is the lowest aside from Italy. The value-added tax is split into a four per cent levy on food and other cost-of-living items and 15 per cent on the rest.

Money is pouring into Dutch pockets at such a rate that many bankers and businessmen are demanding austere anti-inflationary policies which could, in turn, produce recession. The Netherlands has moved up in the last couple of years from seventh place on the league table of British export markets to third position behind the U.S. and West Germany. In 1970 Britain sold roughly £380-million of exports to the Netherlands, equivalent to almost £30 for every Dutch citizen. In return, the Dutch maintained their usual trade surplus by selling £460-million worth of goods to Britain.

Trade with Britain
Although the value of British exports to the Netherlands has risen substantially, Britain's share of total Dutch imports has declined from about eight per cent in 1957 to 6·5 per cent in 1965 and 5·9 per cent in 1970. Considering the advantages enjoyed by Britain's Common Market competitors, notably West Germany, the major Dutch trading partner, this is perhaps not an alarming decrease. But it is one that Britain hopes to reverse on joining the Community.

Prospects for British exporters With the gradual removal of trade barriers, British cars and consumer goods stand to benefit more in the Dutch market than machinery, for capital goods, which account for a very large share of Britain's present sales to the Netherlands, generally carry only a marginal duty of five to seven per cent.

Specifically, British trade officials in The Hague suggest that these items should do well on the Dutch market: pollution control plant (since the Netherlands is to spend large sums on water treatment and solid waste disposal equipment); medical equipment and instruments; scientific instruments; farm machinery; computerised warehousing systems and materials handling equipment of all kinds; do-it-yourself kits and tools; paper and board, and reproduction furniture.

As suggested earlier, the climate for British exports could hardly be better. The Dutch, nevertheless, criticise slow deliveries and become justifiably annoyed with British firms which do not even bother to give sufficient warning or explanation when they cannot deliver on schedule. They would like to see British businessmen come over more often to study the market and they criticise exporters who offer the standard product geared to British tastes instead of what the Dutch buyer wants. They neither want nor expect British businessmen to speak Dutch.

Dutch exporters' prospects in Britain   The Dutch hope to benefit from the dismantling of British import barriers. Economics ministry spokesmen say this will affect industrial goods more than farm products, on which British demand seems steady despite price changes. Obviously, the Dutch hope to capture some of the butter and cheese markets in Britain now enjoyed by New Zealand and Australia, but they hesitate to forecast how soon and by how much present trade patterns will change.

Actually, meat and vegetables produce accounted for less than one-tenth of Dutch exports to Britain in 1970. Petroleum products alone accounted for one-sixth.

Trade with the Irish Republic

The trade picture between Ireland and the Netherlands is dominated by Irish beef cattle. Up to 1966 the Irish enjoyed a steady Dutch market worth about £4-million a year. Then the Common Market levies began to bite and within a few months this trade all but disappeared. At present Ireland is selling only about £100-thousand of cattle to the Dutch a year, primarily for insemination. However, the Dutch consumer boom is beginning to take effect and, once Ireland gets into the Market and the fences come down, there is no reason why it should not regain its old position. Indeed, one Irish diplomat in Holland is privately guessing that the beef cattle market could be worth £10-million a year by 1977. Other promising fields for Irish exports to the Netherlands include lead and zinc ores, peat moss (on which exports to the Dutch are running close to £250-thousand a year), textiles (within narrow limits), crushed stone and gravel (now £500-thousand a year), whisky and leather goods. In reverse, the Netherlands competes with Britain on the Irish market in textiles, plastics and fruit, to list a few examples. As both Britain and Ireland join the Community, traditional British exporters to Ireland will have to look out for the Dutch.

14

BELGIUM AND LUXEMBOURG

Linked in a close economic union over the last half century, the oldest existing merger of its kind, the Kingdom of Belgium and the Grand Duchy of Luxembourg are looking forward to the enlarging of the Common Market to enliven and streamline (rather than boost and 'inflate') their two-way trading with Britain and the other new-comers. They justify these expectations by the fact that in the Common Market of the Six their exports, mainly of finished goods, to their four Market partners have increased from 40 per cent of their output to 67 per cent.

But 'Belux', as the two are sometimes called to distinguish them from 'Benelux' (their younger and looser economic union with the Netherlands), does not expect quite the same spectacular progress in trade with Britain and the three other applicants. The Irish Republic has a limited choice of products. Denmark and Norway are some-what remote geographically and trade with Britain is so well balanced that major changes are not expected. After the failure of the Common Market Six to decide on joint monetary policies in the face of U.S. measures (August, 1971), Belgium and Luxembourg decided to join the Netherlands in floating their currencies so that Benelux became a jointly floating 'mini-bloc'.

The 'language war' which divided Belgium's Flemish and French-speaking (Walloon) populations for many years, appears to be ending, the Belgian legislature having approved 'decentralising' constitutional reforms.

The Belgians are proud that Brussels is the capital of the European Communities and of their impressive European quarter. This has a large star-shaped building, now headquarters for the Commission, in the centre of Schuman Square. Another large headquarters is being built nearby for the Council and its secretariat. The roof of the Commission headquarters has been designed to enable helicopters to land. Enterprising British brewers have opened a pub next door to the Commission. Brussels' claim as permanent capital of the Community (a final decision has yet to be taken on this) is enhanced by the establishment of the North Atlantic Treaty Organisation (NATO) headquarters near the city. There is increasing pressure to end the arrangement under which Luxembourg is an alternative

Community capital: the Council and Commission meet there in June and October. The European (Common Market) Parliament has its administrative offices in Luxembourg and holds its meetings in Strasbourg. The French have just begun to build a new head-quarters for the European Parliament and for the Consultative Assembly of the Council of Europe on the site of the temporary headquarters in Strasbourg. There remain, however, high hopes that the European Parliament and its administration will move to Brussels.

Trade with Britain

In 1970 the Belgium–Luxembourg union exported £170-million worth of goods to Britain, its biggest trading partner outside the Common Market; its imports from Britain totalled £275-million. Britain exported £34-million worth of cars and spare parts for assembly plants in Belgium and Luxembourg in 1970. The Belgians, in the same period, sent to Britain £30-million worth of non-British cars assembled in Belgium.

In 1971 the chief British exports were rough diamonds (both for industry and jewellery) to be cut by world-famous Antwerp diamond cutters. Of the £75-million worth of these diamonds (mostly South African), exported from Britain to Belgium in 1970 £17-million worth were re-exported back to Britain.

Other British exports are chemicals, plastics, textiles, machines, electrical appliances, copper, nickel, lead, iron ore and about £3-million worth a year of gin and whisky.

British exporters' prospects All Britain's industrial exports to Belgium are expected to gain as a result of entry, especially semi-finished goods, machine parts and capital equipment. The two-way flow in cars is expected to continue and there may be a moderate increase in diamond trade.

One member of the British Chamber of Commerce for Belgium and Luxembourg has said: 'British businessmen are rated very highly in Belgium for their integrity', but added: 'Unfortunately they have not a great reputation for delivering goods on time'. He advised British exporters to take into account more the tastes and preferences of the Belgian and Luxembourg natives 'and to abandon forever the take-it-or-leave-it approach'.

Even if a British businessman knows French or Flemish, he is advised to begin the conversation in English. Near the coast and in industrialised Flanders, many businessmen know more English than French. French is in demand in southern and eastern Belgium.

Belgian and Luxembourg exporters' prospects in Britain Belgian biscuits, vegetables (including chicory), and flowers and plants for home decoration are expected to sell better in Britain after entry.

Belgian and Luxembourg exporters are also hoping to develop their exports of goods to other countries, such as Ireland and members of the Commonwealth, by using the experience and know-how of British export merchants.

Main imports into the Belgium–Luxembourg union are the full range of ferrous and non-ferrous metals, machines and electrical appliances, minerals, including coal, petroleum, iron ore and other ores, ore scrap, transport equipment, including cars, other vehicles, rough diamonds, textiles and chemicals.

In 1970 Belgian–Luxembourg imports were £4·74-million, mainly raw materials, semi-finished products and spare parts. Exports totalled £4·84-million, principally finished goods.

Chief suppliers are West Germany, France, the Netherlands, the U.S., Britain, and Italy in that order. Importers are mainly from West Germany, France, the Netherlands, the U.S., Italy and Britain.

Trade with the Irish Republic
More Irish cattle is expected to be exported to Belgium and Luxembourg; however, the forecast is that the bulk of Irish exports will continue to go to Britain. In 1970 Irish exports to Belgium and Luxembourg totalled just over £5-million including lead ore, fish and cattle.

15

DENMARK

Twenty-five years ago, Denmark shifted its emphasis to industry. As a result, industrial exports outstripped agricultural sales for the first time in 1964 and are now about 65 per cent of its total export trade. The switch was accelerated by what the Danes regarded as unsatisfactory prices for their farm produce in Britain, their principal export market.

After ten years of balance of payments difficulties, Denmark imposed an import surcharge in October, 1971. High cost of industrialisation was given as one cause of the imbalance; but it is also true that Denmark has been living beyond its means, thus encouraging spiralling costs and prices. The wages system includes built-in automatic increases to compensate for increasing prices. Private consumption has increased by 21 per cent in the past five years, measured in real values.

The new Danish light industries have helped to increase exports by two-hundred per cent in ten years.

Trade with Britain
Denmark's application for membership of the Common Market depended on British entry. Britain provides its principal market for farm produce and is its third largest supplier after West Germany and Sweden. Denmark is Britain's 12th largest market and imported £253·73-million worth of British goods in 1970, including petroleum and its products, transport equipment, non-electric machinery and textiles. Britain's imports from Denmark totalled £259·6-million and included mainly food and such products as non-electrical and electrical machinery, furniture and clothing.

British exporters' prospects　　Britain will have to face more competition in the Danish market since it will lose the protection if had as a fellow member of the European Free Trade Association (EFTA).

British exporters, however, will continue to benefit from the generally good reputation British goods enjoy in Denmark. A major British export drive for capital goods is planned in 1972 on the assumption that Denmark's industry is now ripe for sophisticated equipment, such as machine tools, packaging machinery, metalworking machinery and shipbuilding equipment. There is also a good potential market for agricultural machinery and for scientific controlling and measuring machinery as well as medical and hospital (patient monitoring) equipment. British exporters are advised to keep in close touch with their Danish agents. There are no language difficulties as many Danes speak better English than the British and enjoy speaking it.

Danish exporters' prospects in Britain Danish exporters are not afraid of increased competition from the Common Market Six on the British market. They are not predicting which of their exports are likely to succeed in Britain if she joins the Market but are confident of success. The 20 largest Danish exporters which now provide 35 per cent of total industrial exports provided five per cent just ten years ago.

There is very little trade between Denmark and the Irish Republic.

16

NORWAY

The Norwegians are among the most popular of the Nordic peoples, especially in Britain. Dependent on the sea, Norway's fleet, 19·7-million gross tons, is the fourth largest in the world and 97 per cent of it is used in foreign trade. It is situated on the northern flank of NATO, beyond the Arctic circle where it has a common frontier with the Soviet Union.

The strategic importance of applying special safeguards for farmers and fishermen in the north to prevent the depopulation of the frontier areas was frequently stressed in the Common Market negotiations. Although the Norwegians have recently struck oil in the North Sea, speculation on future production has been cautious.

Trade with Britain
Britain is Norway's most important export market and her third largest supplier. British exports to Norway, amounting to £189·3-million in 1970, included in order of their importance: transport equipment, non-electrical machinery, petroleum and its products, iron and steel, textiles, electrical machinery. It has 14th place in our export markets.

Britain's imports from Norway, totalling £182·8-million in 1970, were in order of importance: non-ferrous metals, pulp and paper, iron and steel, metalliferous ores and scrap metal, fish and chemicals.

British exporters' prospects　British sales have a good chance of being maintained and possibly improving, even though our exporters lose the special protection they had from their partnership in EFTA.

In the new enlarged Common Market, however, British exporters must offer competitive prices and qualities, including service facilities to follow up sales. They must also offer realistic delivery dates (Norwegians are sticklers for punctuality). In 1971 this seemed to give a slight advantage to the West Germans. Norwegian importers say the West German delivery dates can be relied upon. This does not mean that the bulk of British goods is not delivered on time; but Norway is a small nation and news of every delay spreads and may well hamper a new contract with a new customer later. Therefore British exporters should inform customers well in advance of any unavoidable delays and certainly not leave it until the last moment.

Adequate warning helps the customer to adjust his own plans, thus reducing irritation.

British exporters are advised to visit their agents in Norway at least once a year. They should not only go to Oslo but try to visit their prospective customers in other parts of Norway. Many big plants are near hydro-electric power stations and have no offices in Oslo. A personal visit usually serves but travelling takes up much time despite domestic air services. Norwegian roads are narrow and winding and include many ferry trips across the fjords so that 125 miles is considered a day's drive in the summer.

The British exporter will have no language difficulties since most Norwegians know and enjoy speaking English. However, their affection for Britain does not influence their commercial dealings.

Visiting Britons should note that Oslo's hotel accommodation is very limited. Another warning: the Norwegians morally disapprove of alcohol (although their schnapps is world-renowned) and drinks are, therefore, expensive and not served at all on Saturdays or Sundays (and public holidays). This rule also applies to residents.

Norwegian exporters' prospects in Britain   As the bulk of Norway's exports to Britain are raw materials, its exporters do not expect increased competition from the Common Market Six in the enlarged Market. Trade is likely to be much as before. As with imports, Norway's exports amount to approximately 35 per cent of its GNP, usually with an import surplus.

Norway's request for a special protocol to meet its fisheries' problem was met by an agreement for a 12-mile limit along much of the west and north coast for Norwegian fishermen during a 10-year transition period. It promised 'special consideration' which could mean prolonging the transition beyond 1983.

Fishing and fish processing constitute the economic basis for the population settled along the extensive coastal areas of Norway. The industry is based on exploiting stocks of fish in the waters adjacent to the coast. For these reasons, and due to the short distances from the fishing harbours to the fishing banks, the fisheries industry has evolved a special structure. The fishing vessels, primarily small, number about 36-thousand and are manned by some 40-thousand men. The processing plants are distributed along the entire coast.

Norway's topographical conditions result in high production costs for many agricultural products. The farms are scattered and mainly consist of small freehold units. It was necessary, therefore, to apply national support measures to secure an adequate standard of living for the farmers.

17

BRITAIN IN EUROPE

Britain's entry into the European Communities can be the beginning, in the view of most of our political leaders and of the Six, of a new renaissance—a great step towards increasing the stability, prosperity and quality of life for the peoples of Western Europe.

Not even the most ardent supporters of the wider Common Market, in Britain or the Six, claim that it is certain that it will be. It will be an opportunity, for the Six and for Britain and the other countries that have agreed to go in, to make a fresh start together to complete and greatly strengthen the Community which, in many respects, is still little more than a base or framework. Joseph Luns, who, during 20 years as Dutch Foreign Minister, has done as much as any British minister to open the way for entry, and others have repeatedly warned that the benefits which Britain and its partners receive from the enlarged Community will depend very much on whether there is a dedication to the European venture; whether we intend, not only to profit from the Market, but to use it as a basis for a fuller political union. The British are, they believe, in a situation which is in some ways comparable to that of 1940, in the sense that we cannot hope to meet the challenge of the Market without maximum unity and effort at home. They emphasise that, although the Community has proved its value, it remains a fragile instrument. The approach which Britain decides to take to its future development, especially in the political field, could make or break it.

Prime Minister Heath made it clear during the debate on principle in October, 1971, that, although determined to retain the right to exercise the veto in Brussels decision-making, his government would be willing to move cautiously towards closer political co-operation with its future partners. If the Labour Party were returned to power and attempted to withdraw or change the Market into another European Free Trade Association, it is generally believed that the Community would face the worst crisis in its history. The view in Brussels is that Labour would not attempt to break with the Market, one of the chief reasons being that dislocation of the Market could mean a return to nationalist trading policies causing mass unemployment.

Britain and the Six have been moving closer together in ways which

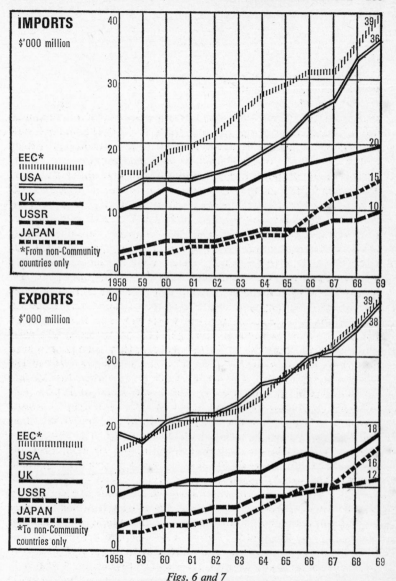

Figs. 6 and 7
The relative strength of the EEC as a trade group when compared to other leading import–export countries. British entry would establish the Market as the largest trading entity and greatly strengthen its voice in international affairs (*Source:* EEC Commission).

mean that, to an increasing extent, they are acting as if it were already a member of the Market. The Six have, for instance, invited the Chancellor of the Exchequer, Anthony Barber, to join them in attempts to work out common monetary policies. The invitation followed the clash between West Germany and France in mid-1971 over the German decision to float the mark and the failure of the Six to agree among themselves on how to react to American trade restrictions and other measures. After President Nixon announced the measures, the British government arranged to begin detailed discussion with Nixon's envoys. As they were arriving in London, British monetary experts cancelled plans to meet them first and, instead, began talks with monetary officials of the Six.

These talks led to what is regarded by the Six as a 'watershed' meeting in Brussels of the finance ministers, who were holding an emergency session to discuss the currency crisis. The seven ministers agreed that they should continue close consultations, not only in their own immediate national interests, but so that they would all be better placed after British entry to co-operate in moving towards a Western European economic and monetary union.

The fate of one of the cornerstones of the Market, the common agricultural policy (CAP), depended to a great extent on the outcome of these consultations. This was because the changes in the value of the dollar, the mark and other currencies threatened to create havoc in the CAP's farm prices system, so much so that there was a danger that the common agricultural market would disintegrate into separate national markets resulting from controls on the flow of foodstuffs across common frontiers. The Six were hoping to form, with Britain, a united front in future talks with the U.S. on world currency problems. Closely linked with this were the efforts the Six were making to avoid a trade war with the U.S. over what the Americans regarded as the 'dangerously protectionist' policies resulting from CAP and a helpful trade agreement was reached early in 1972.

European political union
Another way in which Britain has begun to act as if it were already part of the Community is the agreement under which Sir Alec Douglas-Home, Foreign Secretary, has begun consultations with the foreign ministers of the Six and the other applicants for Market membership in the framework of the Davignon Committee (see Chapter 1, Origins of the Common Market). There appeared to be a consensus among the ten governments to use the Davignon meetings to prepare an agenda and outline proposals on foreign policy for a summit meeting of their heads of government.

French representatives have revived parts of a plan put forward by Gaullist France in the early 1960s. Under this there would be regular foreign policy meetings of the Market member states, first at the level of foreign office political directors, then at the foreign ministerial level and finally at a head of government level. The aim would be a gradual approach to create a single European foreign policy, first perhaps in the Middle East for which an outline plan has already been tabled, and, at a later stage, in the other key areas of international politics. There would be decision-making institutions for foreign policy which would function in much the same way that the Market institutions function to establish common economic and trade policies. A common foreign policy was intended as a step to a Western European political union. The leaders of the smaller members of the Market, particularly Dr. Luns of the Netherlands and M. Spaak of Belgium, feared that they would be forced to accept common policies imposed by France and West Germany. They refused to implement the political union plan until Britain could be brought in to maintain the balance.

Now that Britain is expected to join, the Dutch, Belgians and others favour what they call a *relance politique* ('relaunching' of the political union idea). French representatives have suggested that the head of government presiding over the summit meeting (the chairmanship would rotate regularly among members) should act for all ten countries in direct talks with other national heads of government on monetary and trade problems. When the founders of the European Communities drew up their first plan in the late 1940s, they proposed that one of their first steps should be to establish political union. This idea was eventually abandoned when Britain refused to join the Six. The wheel of European unity is, with the prospect of British entry, now turning full circle.

Progress on political union may well depend on the future development of East–West relations. Another major world crisis could lead to the political 'relaunching'. The British government will no doubt prefer to allow ample time, initially, for digesting the integration involved by joining the Common Market before moving on to new fields.

European defence co-operation

Fears that the United States might suddenly withdraw large numbers of troops from Europe have led the Brussels planners to re-examine plans put forward by the founders (and supported by Mr. Churchill in the 1940s) for integrating the forces of Western European countries in a European defence community. The plans, drawn up by the federalists mainly, called for a European government with federal powers. It is agreed among the governments of the ten prospective members of the enlarged Market that the defence community plans cannot be accepted as they stand. There is, however, growing support for using the Western European Union organisation, created by Britain and the Six partly to oversee German rearmament, as the 'defence wing' of the European Community. In France and the Netherlands, hopes have been expressed that Mr. Heath will eventually revive an idea he stressed when in Opposition, for a joint Anglo-French nuclear force. There have also been suggestions that the U.S. MacMahon Act of 1946, preventing Britain from discussing the most important features of its nuclear 'knowhow' with European countries, should be abrogated. In the latest exchanges between Western European governments, emphasis has been placed on the need to reduce the cost of weapons by joint production on an European-wide scale.

It is significant that one of the most respected men in the Commission, Jean-François Deniau of France, who is spoken of as a future Commission president, has stressed the need for a 'European identity' in defence as well as foreign affairs and the monetary field. His summing up of the philosophy of the Community, often quoted in Brussels, is: 'Constructive political developments will be thought of when full economic unity has been achieved in the Common Market. The political aspects stem from the size of the economic commitments . . . *If we wish to go further then we must go much further* . . . It will doubtless prove to be both possible and necessary to go faster and further.' (The italics are M. Deniau's.) The most that has been done so far on European defence co-operation has been the 'Euro-group', comprising the European members of NATO. As in the case of political union the functionalist-minded British, while frequently stressing the need for closer defence co-operation in speeches, will probably move slowly in this field unless jolted by a new crisis. Brussels officials hope however that, once Britain has joined, it will gradually adopt a position of looking further ahead than the latest source of tension or the next election.

CONSTITUTIONAL CONSEQUENCES

The constitutional implications for Britain and the Commonwealth of signing the Treaty of Rome would be:

Crown and Constitution The Queen's constitutional position as head of state and of the Commonwealth would be unchanged just as the monarchies of the countries already in the Common Market are unaffected.

Commonwealth As the Queen is the link between Britain and the Commonwealth, entry into the Market requires no changes in the constitution of the Commonwealth members or in their ties with Britain in the many organisations such as those for technical aid and education. British trade agreements with the Commonwealth will in future be negotiated in accordance with Community rules but British ministers and officials will be in Brussels to see that the rules are sensibly implemented. The most important of these agreements are those which safeguard New Zealand's exports of dairy products to Britain, and ultimately to the wider Market, and sugar exports from the developing Commonwealth.

The entry terms mean that membership, in addition to uniting a large part of Western Europe, will link the greater part of the Commonwealth with the enlarged Market. The Treaty of Accession therefore constitutes one of the historic acts of political unity between sovereign states. Commonwealth conferences will be held as before. The fact that African countries, formerly governed by Britain and France, are under the entry agreements to be linked in Brussels by common organisations, economic and political, may help to unite them.

The Government Apart from the losses of sovereignty involved in establishing economic and commercial links with the Six, the national government will be free of Community restraint. Nevertheless, failure by a government to act constructively in Brussels could bring about its downfall in national elections. Most of the Six believe that if any of their governments tried to undermine the Community, that government would fall.

The Treasury As explained earlier in this chapter, it will be consulting Britain's Market partners, in fact has already begun to do so, on broad policy issues. Britain could devalue the pound as easily as West Germany and other Market countries have floated or otherwise adjusted their currencies.

Department of Trade and Industry Under the entry terms, it would lose most of its tariff-negotiating functions. The minister would be heard in the Council of Ministers and in the decision-making bodies in Brussels when tariffs were fixed. There would be two Britons on the Commission acting for the Community in tariff negotiations.

Foreign and Commonwealth Office This would keep complete control over foreign policies, despite the early moves which have been aimed at harmonising the policies of member states. That any member state can follow its own national foreign policy has been repeatedly shown since the Market was formed, the striking recent example being West Germany's *Ostpolitik*.

Home Office   The only policy under its jurisdiction which will be affected is immigration control. Market membership will mean that workers from member states will not be required to have labour permits as of next January.

Ministry of Agriculture and Fisheries   Although conforming to the common policies of the Market, it will be responsible for implementing them and reviewing the needs of Britain's farmers and fishermen.

Defence and Service Ministries   These would in no sense come under the control of Community institutions unless Britain and her partners decide unanimously to move towards closer defence co-operation.

Ministry for the Environment   The Community is already pre-occupied with the effects of industrial development on the environment. The British minister will discuss plans with the Six for common rules to protect the countryside and historic buildings.

Ministry of Education   The Six are planning a European University in Florence and a number of other joint educational projects. English, French, Italian, German and Dutch will be the University's official languages, with English and French as working languages. Plans were approved for exchanges of teachers and students.

Parliament   It will retain its sovereignty, except in decisions on tariffs, agriculture and other aspects of the economy that are involved in Market planning. The Treaty contains no binding clause to the effect that the Brussels institutions may overrule any national legislature. Britain and Italy have agreed to attempt to strengthen the European Parliament which can dismiss the Commission, but cannot challenge the decisions of any national legislature. The resulting dilemma is that much policy formulation and implementation will continue in Brussels without adequate democratic supervision. But to strengthen the European Parliament by having its members elected by direct universal suffrage could affect the stature of the British Parliament. One justification for electing special Euro-MPs could be that, in the enlarged Community, European legislative business might become time-consuming enough to merit full-time members.

Heated arguments developed during the run-up to British entry over the extent to which Parliament could oppose a Community regulation agreed upon by the ministers at the Brussels Council. What seems clear is that failure by Parliament to approve a Brussels decision could provoke a political crisis. To counter such a crisis, great care would be taken in the many preliminary discussions of a proposal in Brussels to ensure that nothing likely to provoke an adverse vote at home would be done. British representatives have said they would prefer to approach this aspect of the Common Market pragmatically through the evolution of a new series of checks and balances.

The Civil Service By next January, assuming British entry, a 'little Whitehall' will be installed in Brussels consisting of a few dozen important officials at first but ultimately expanding to nearly one-thousand. A drive has begun in Whitehall to encourage both diplomats and civil servants in all departments to learn one or, if possible, two Community languages. French and German are the most important but a knowledge of Italian or Dutch could be very helpful in the Brussels negotiating sessions. Britain's Civil Service is expected to play an important role in the Community, an expectation based on its reputed skill and efficiency among Continental civil servants who would be their colleagues in the Community's administration.

The French have provided some of the finest civil servants in Brussels. This in itself is reason enough for choosing top men to send to Brussels. The Six were impressed by Britain's team of officials under Geoffrey Rippon which negotiated the entry terms, including his deputy, Sir Con O'Neill of the Foreign Office, Raymond Bell of the Treasury, Freddie Kearns (Agriculture), G. R. Denman (Trade and Industry) and John Robinson (Foreign Office). This represented a good cross section of civil servants. Their qualities most highly rated by Community officials were forthrightness (especially Mr. Kearns') in stating Britain's case, a sense of humour and, above all, a capacity to keep the sessions as short as possible by doing their homework and not wasting words at the negotiating table. In such ways the British Civil Service could be especially helpful in Community institutions which tend to waste time on unnecessary wrangling.

Some British negotiators will continue to watch over Community negotiations in Brussels after entry, if only because very few of their colleagues in London even begin to understand Community institutions and problems.

Michael Palliser, the new Ambassador to the European Communities, leads the 'first wave' of permanently based British Eurocrats-designate in Brussels, where he is highly regarded. After taking up his post, he began to join in discussions with the Six on the Market's policies and plans very much as if he had already become Britain's Permanent Representative, the post he will hold in the Market's institutions after British entry. The Six were pleased when, on arrival in Brussels, he made a gesture of friendship by stressing that he expected that French would still be much used as a working language of the Community.

If Britain joins, Mr. Palliser's post may gradually become the most important in the Diplomatic Service. The Italians look upon their London ambassador as holding the key position in their diplomatic service during the next few years on the grounds that they attach the greatest importance to Britain's initial approach to the Community.

The Courts British decisions could, in a limited number of cases, be overruled by the Community's Court of Justice in Luxembourg, but only in the fields which the British Parliament decides upon, such as rules to ensure fair competition between firms. Additionally, the Community's legal system generally will be strengthened by the addition of British judges and lawyers.

There will be no changes in British criminal law. Habeas Corpus will continue as will the legal premise that a man is innocent until proven guilty.

The Police Free movement of people between Britain and the Continent is expected to lead to even closer co-operation than previously between European police forces. One possible result of entry will be the need to investigate new kinds of fraud due to the Community regulations on trade in such things as food. Authorities in the Six are hoping that closer links between the countries of Western Europe will help to co-ordinate efforts to reduce drug trafficking and the production and sale of drugs for illegal use. President Pompidou has made proposals for joint action.

It is clear from this survey of the likely impact of entry on Whitehall and of British officials' impact on the Community that the link with the Six can be realised smoothly and efficiently. Britain will have no difficulty in defending her interests at every stage in the Brussels decision-making. Gradually over the years, it seems certain that the Community system will achieve a flexibility and pragmatism which will owe much to the British participation.

EVERYDAY CONSEQUENCES

If Britain joins the Market most Britons will, for the first few years and perhaps longer, find that the life of the country and their own lives, will go on very much as before. This was the experience of the peoples of the Six. Indeed millions in the member countries scarcely realised until late in the 1960s that they were in the Common Market.

Press reports of the wrangling of the Six over intricate technical matters such as sluice-gate prices were tucked away on the financial pages and the only tangible signs that anything had changed were the increase in prosperity and fewer restrictions at common frontiers. As recently as 1968 it was possible to find people living in Savoie who had never heard of the Common Market and in Strasbourg people who thought that Britain had always been a member. As the only people in Europe who have really debated the Common Market issue, the British know far more about it than the peoples who have lived with it for years.

An incident that did more to attract public attention to the Brussels institutions than any of the long Council sessions was the demonstration staged in Brussels by angry farmers against the low farm prices, at the beginning of which demonstrators drove three cows up the marble steps of the Palais de Congrès and straight into the Council chamber on the second floor where agricultural ministers of the Six were meeting. Since then, Common Market farm prices have increased. The Irish also once staged a demonstration before the conference building as Ireland's Foreign Minister, Patrick Hillery, arrived for the first negotiating sessions.

The national spirit of the peoples of the Six remains as strong as ever. Very few of them would dream of adopting the nationality of any of the others. However, the peoples are becoming closer, notably the French and the Germans, the result in part of the friendship policy instituted by President de Gaulle. The worst Franco-German incidents so far have been the clashes between France's Finance Minister, Giscard d'Estaing, and West Germany's Karl Schiller during which Giscard was understood to have said at an 'ultra-secret' session that France had no intention of taking lessons on anything from the Germans. At the height of the quarrel with Prof. Schiller, Giscard suddenly rang him up and they then agreed to avoid personal remarks during their Council exchanges. This, in view of Prof. Schiller's somewhat caustic way of negotiating, was considered no small triumph for the Community spirit.

The verdict of most Community people is that their countries have profited on the whole in a material sense from the economic dynamism, without in any way being tied down to any objectionable form of control from Brussels. Opinion polls (despite their reputation as unpredictable guides) in all Market countries reveal a pro-Market view.

These examples of how entry into the Market may eventually affect the people of Britain, their work and leisure and general way of life are based on what is happening in the Six and on estimates of the effects of the terms of British entry:

Industry: management and workers The challenge of the Common Market for both sides of industry (see Chapter 3) is a major point among Britain's friends in Brussels. They are urging government and trade union leaders to do much more to bring about a change in enterprise and initiative. Industrialists in the Six point out that even Italy, less developed than Britain and having to send goods greater distances, can deliver factory equipment and similar products to this country more economically than they can be made here. Even when it is known that British firms can supply goods at lower prices, orders often go to firms on the Continent because they have a better reputation for punctual delivery. The Six were surprised that, as it was preparing to join the Common Market, Britain decided to go back to British time so that, during the busy winter months, they were one hour ahead. Firms on the Continent also noted that British offices begin work much later than many of their offices so that much valuable time is lost in doing business with the British.

The essence of the challenge, as it is seen by firms in Market countries, is that the negotiated entry terms will, assuming that Britain joins, give British industry two or three years in which to acquire a reputation for delivery of goods in sufficient quantity and at the right price to make the most of the common industrial market. Britain stands to receive the advantages of the large market, from the rapid lowering of industrial tariffs, before it shoulders the full burden of agricultural costs of entry resulting from the more gradual application of the whole of the common agricultural policy. If British industry 'delivers the goods', the farm bill can, the Six say, be easily met. If not, then there would be balance of payments and other difficulties.

The wage–price spiral's contribution to inflation should be obvious to all interest groups. What is relevant is that wage demands become excessive (and increase prices) when production does not keep pace. This warning, issued often in Britain, has been re-iterated in the Community.

One labour issue on which little progress has been made in Market countries is that of equal pay for women, provided for in the Rome Treaty. Unions in Britain and on the Continent could usefully campaign to see that this ruling be more consistently implemented.

European socialists such as West German Chancellor Brandt and the Netherlands' Dr. Mansholt, head of the common agricultural system, have advised British labour leaders, parliamentary and trades union, to end their opposition to entry into the Market and to discuss its advantages with their followers. It is pointed out that even Communist parties on the Continent, under great pressure from Moscow to oppose the Common Market, are giving it their support and are sending their MPs to its Parliament.

The housewife It is certain that food prices will rise in Britain's shops, if only because food has been cheaper in Britain in the past because of the large amounts imported from Australia and New Zealand. Although a large part of New Zealand's dairy exports to Britain will continue under a preferential tariff for a while, by the late 1970s they will be sold at higher prices because they will be subject to levies in the ports. Food prices in the shops will no longer be subsidised and preference will be given to food produced in the Common Market countries, notably France, instead of, say, to food from Australia.

Food prices have already been rising in Britain, however, and the gap which has to be closed between British and Common Market levels is narrower than it was in the mid-1960s. Prices, as measured by the retail price index, have risen from 6·3 per cent in 1969 to 7·7 per cent in 1970 and another 12 per cent to September, 1971.

Treasury estimates suggest that food prices will rise by about 2½p in the £ each year during the transition period to full membership, or about 15 per cent over the period, in addition to any other increases which might occur. This would equal an increase of about ½p in the £ in the total cost of living, which would be too small to have any real influence on wage claims or on industrial costs and the competitive position of British manufacturers.

Judging by the experience of the Six, housewives will find a much greater variety of goods in British shops, such as Continental food delicacies, kitchen appliances and clothing.

Living costs in Britain, again as measured by the retail price index, have risen rapidly and to unaccustomed levels over the last 18 months. They rose 5·4 per cent in 1969, 6·3 per cent in 1970 and by September, 1971, were still showing an annual increase of almost 10 per cent although the rate was decreasing. This upward trend in living costs is slowing against a background of price restraint measures and tax changes although not sufficiently to produce the hope of returning to the former low rate of increase.

Prospects are that inflation will further narrow the gap with Common Market living costs and, while uncomfortable, provide some cushion for the agricultural policy's effect on food prices.

The professions Ultimately under the provisions of the Rome Treaty, members of the professions can establish themselves with equal rights in any member state. National restrictions preventing this are due to be removed on the basis of directives drafted by the Common Market Commission's staff, working in close contact with national government departments and with professional and other organisations. The drafts are then to be submitted by the Commission to the Council of Ministers, which, after adopting them, refer them to the European Parliament and the Economic and Social Committee.

Most of the professions are still unaffected by Common Market rules because of the wide differences in required professional qualifications, methods of training and privileges in the various member states. In 1971 the Market Council had before it proposals made by the Commission for applying the rules to doctors, dentists, veterinary surgeons, opticians and nurses but no decision had been taken. The proposals included directives regarding the manufacture of drugs and medicines.

The rules have also not been applied to the legal and technical professions. Directives were being prepared by the Commission for tax consultants. Under the heading of 'cultural professions', some restrictions have been removed from some sectors of the film industry. A draft directive on the press was being examined by the Council and proposals were being prepared regarding recreation services, including sports instructors.

The Council is also considering directives from the Commission on bankers, insurance agents, chemists and architects.

Explaining why relatively little progress has been made in 'liberalising the professions', as it is called in Brussels jargon, the Commission says one reason is lack of staff. Although there are some 9-thousand staff in the Commission headquarters and related departments (equal in size to a large British government department), the Commission, under pressure of negotiations and administration in other fields, can only spare a few officials to prepare directives covering the professions. Another cause of delay is the difficulty in gaining the acceptance by each member state that the required qualifications and diplomas in the other states are equivalent to their own.

Scientists and technologists The Six attach great importance to the contribution which British scientists and technologists can make to joint research projects launched in European institutions, especially in the field of advanced technology. A European patent system has been drawn up by representatives of the Six and of European countries outside the Market. This will make it possible to protect inventions in a single European Patent Office instead of having to go to eight or ten different national offices.

Businessmen Industrialists, shopkeepers, hoteliers, owners of theatres, cinemas, bars, public houses, and other businessmen have, under the Treaty, the right to establish themselves anywhere in the

Common Market. The Council has adopted a directive aimed at co-ordinating company law (publication of particulars, validity of commitments and nullity of association). Two draft directives are also being submitted to the Council on mergers between companies of the same country and maintenance or changes in companies' capital. Britain is being consulted on the creation of a European company law. The goal is to help businessmen in the running of their businesses on a European instead of on a national basis; with the help of common rules for cross-frontier amalgamations.

Commuters Many people in the Six commute daily across common frontiers and special rules are being made to help them. Most of the travellers between member states do not feel that they are going abroad. An identity card is frequently shown instead of a passport. There will be many more British commuters to the Continent as more British firms cross the Channel. One of the most enterprising airlines in the Six has for some time been running a service of what it calls 'Common Market commuters'. Community officials themselves find that the only way to maintain adequate contact with national politics while meeting their Common Market colleagues is to commute regularly between their capitals and Brussels or Luxembourg. After Brussels had become the Market capital, train services and the road to Paris were greatly improved. Eurocrats find they can get home almost as quickly and certainly much more comfortably than many who commute between London and the suburbs.

Motorists The Commission has tabled plans for reducing frontier formalities such as the control of the international (green) insurance card. Co-operation among the Six has led to improvement in roads between them and to plans for a network of north–south and east–west E (Europe) roads spanning Western Europe.

Safety standards on Continental roads are being improved by common rules for road signs and for such things as signalling equipment on cars.

Innkeepers As Britain harmonises its policies with those of the Six in many other fields it may well be encouraged to bring its licensing laws into line with those of the Common Market. Brussels planners say it is possible that some Continental liquors will eventually be on sale in Britain at lower prices. Wine exporters have long predicted that *vin ordinaire* is likely to be cheaper once Britain joins but representatives in Brussels have recently said that this is not certain.

Holidaymakers Despite the rules for allowing free movement of goods across common frontiers, national authorities continue to restrict the amount of liquor or of scent, tobacco and luxuries generally which tourists can bring home duty-free. Britain is expected to adopt the rules in this sector, recently agreed on by the Six, under which the following are allowed to pass through customs duty-free: 400 cigarettes or cigars; up to 1 litre whisky, gin or brandy or 3 litres champagne or 4 litres wine; unlimited scent.

Pet owners The quarantine rules in Britain designed to prevent outbreaks of rabies will remain unchanged.

Pensioners To counteract the effects of higher living costs on persons who live on fixed incomes and therefore cannot benefit from the higher earnings resulting from the Common Market, the government has said it will take 'whatever measures are necessary to cushion the impact upon pensioners and those least able to bear them'.

Youth The European Parliament of the Six has adopted a recommendation for setting up a European Youth Office which would function in much the same way as the Franco-German Youth Office. The purpose would be to encourage exchange visits between many more young people in the member countries. Article 50 of the Rome Treaty provides that Market states should follow a common policy for exchanging young workers.

Immigrants The Rome Treaty provides that nationals of all member states are, under the free movement of labour rules, able to move to the other member states and take jobs there as if they were citizens. Member governments are entitled to define their nationals. The British definition submitted to the Six in 1971 was: 'Citizens of the United Kingdom and Colonies or British subjects not possessing that citizenship or the citizenship of any other Commonwealth country or territory, who, in either case, have the right of abode in the United Kingdom.'

THE FUTURE

Whether British entry into the Market will mark the beginning of a new renaissance in Europe is a matter of some concern.

Britain's new partners note somewhat anxiously that British public opinion polls still show a considerable number of doubters and that there is a danger that the majority mustered in the House of Commons in favour of entry might dissipate during voting this year (1972) on the consequential legislation (required to bring parts of British law and practice into line with the Community system). They hope that, as has happened in their own countries, the British public will swing strongly and favour the Market once concentration ceases on the disadvantages of the various sectors and realises, perhaps soon after entry, that these will be outweighed by the advantages for the country as a whole.

Despite the nationalistic and self-interested 'what's-in-it for me?' attitude shown by many in Britain, a surprisingly large number of people at all levels have accepted that the Community, with all its faults, could become an instrument for ensuring that the best of European civilisation is used to keep the peace and reduce poverty. This was repeatedly emphasised in speeches by various leaders of all parties during the Common Market debate which ended on October 28 with the House of Commons resolving by 356 votes to 244 (majority 112):

> 'That this House approves Her Majesty's Government's decision of principle to join the European Communities on the basis of the arrangements which have been negotiated.'

Representatives of the Six, observing from the Commons galleries, said the speeches and the vote had convinced them that Britain was at last coming to understand what the Community was all about and that it was ready to join wholeheartedly in building not only a larger Common Market but a political Europe. (They noted in the final stages of the debate inside and outside the Commons that the price of butter which has led to so much wrangling and so many doubts was scarcely mentioned.)

The crux of the economic case for entry, as presented by the government and supported by many of Labour's leaders, was not economic prospects for large British firms in the Common Market or technology or even the rate of growth, important though all these aspects are, but ensuring that Britain was in the best possible position to influence far-reaching economic decisions. These decisions, on whether there should be protectionist or liberal trading policies, will soon be made by the major economic powers, notably the United States. Britain must work in concert with the rest of Europe to ensure a satisfactory outcome to negotiations on the reform of the world monetary system and on world trade, for it would be vulnerable to protectionist pressure if the resulting new financial and trading system was not achieved.

The need for a united Western Europe to use the Community to exert influence on the U.S. cannot be separated entirely from the security of Britain and the Community. An Atlantic alliance is still vital for the defence of Western Europe but, as Mr. Heath has said, there can be no doubt of the growing pressures on Europe to consolidate its own defence position. The decision on British entry could vitally affect the balance of forces in the modern world for many years to come.

Now, following China's entry into the United Nations and signs that the U.S. has accepted China's role in the world and moves towards disarmament, there is a greater need for a single European foreign policy backed by a closely integrated defence system. In this, Britain can assume a new and decisive role. Sir Alec Douglas-Home has already begun talks with his foreign ministerial counterparts of the Six on the co-ordination of an approach to the Soviet Union. This would entail mutual and balanced force reductions in Europe and detailed plans for economic co-operation with the countries of Eastern Europe.

As a member of the Market, Britain would join her partners at a summit meeting of heads of government to settle the European approach to these changes. Failure to join would not prevent a summit meeting from taking decisions which would affect Britain as well as the greater part of Western Europe. Prime Minister Heath concluded in his speech during the debate on principle: 'I want Britain as a member of a Europe which is united politically and which will enjoy lasting peace and the greater security which would ensue.' European observers in the gallery noted that these were the phrases used by the founders of the Community in the 1950s and by Chancellor Brandt and President Pompidou as they opened the door to Britain, twenty years later.

They were further impressed by the vigour of the closing phase of the debate. They saw this as a foretaste of the great contribution Britain would make, as a member of the Community to its European Parliament in Strasbourg.

On January 26, 1972, the government published the European Communities Bill (see Appendix 4) that would enable Britain to fulfill the obligations and exercise the rights conferred by membership in the three Communities. This was criticised on grounds of what were called the unprecedented powers the Bill conferred on the minister, notably Clause 2, which gives the force of law in the United Kingdom to present and future Community law. In the House of Commons voting, the government's majority fell to eight, but the Bill was expected to be approved later in the year in time for entry on January 1, 1973. The Queen's official visit to France, arranged for May, 1972, was welcomed by the French as 'deepening the entente cordiale'.

This fresh start in Anglo-French relations which augurs well for Britain's future in the Community is a direct result of the Community system. At a crucial stage in the British entry negotiations, when it was still not certain that the French would grant reasonable entry terms, Chancellor Brandt and Dr. Luns of the Netherlands urged President Pompidou to help Britain into the Market, instead of

prolonging the cross-Channel bickering which had gone on since
President de Gaulle clashed with Winston Churchill during the
Second World War. Without the Community system, West Germany
would almost certainly have hesitated to urge a closer understanding
between the French and the British because of fears that one or other
might return to the old balance of power tactics. In the enlarged
Community, any or no combination of the three powers could occur.
Such situations have arisen at every stage of the Community's
development and there will be many more of them. The important
difference, say Brussels Eurocrats, will be that Britain and the others
will be aiming at a Community balance of power and not the uneasy
and often short-lived balance arising from one country's self-
interested action. The Eurocrats were not dismayed by the difficulties
in launching the economic and monetary union. To them it was an
immense achievement even to have agreed to attempt its formation.
Serious difficulties on currency, policy and timing were not sufficient
reason to doubt the whole Community system. M. Schumann
pointed out during his London talks that, although France and West
Germany were still far apart on monetary policies and on tactics to
be used in the approach to a European security conference, Walter
Scheel, the West German Foreign Minister, had said at a recent
meeting of the Six foreign ministers that he felt certain a compromise
could be found. M. Schumann stressed that despite their differences
about money France, in turn, remained a firm supporter of West
Germany's *Ostpolitik*.

West Germany then agreed to join France and the other Market
countries in rejecting an American protest to the Six over their plan
for special trading links with European Free Trade Association
countries remaining outside the Market. These 'non-candidates'
were being offered free trade with the Common Market for a large
part of their industrial exports. (They are: Austria, Finland, Iceland,
Portugal, Sweden and Switzerland.) The U.S. claimed that the
industrial free trade arrangement would gravely undermine its
trade with the non-candidates. The Six in their reply insisted
that it conformed with GATT and that American allegations were
unjustified. This in itself was regarded by Brussels Eurocrats as
a major political act by the Community and as an illustration
of how, when facing external difficulties, it could transcend internal
wrangling.

Another illustration of this was a sharp warning the Six agreed
to deliver to Denmark, whose negotiations minister, Ivar Norgaard,
had rejected as finally binding the economic and monetary and social
policies of the Community and insisted that Denmark had to

maintain its commitments under the Nordic Treaty. The Six quickly decided on a Note telling him that Denmark must abide by the economic and monetary policies and, though the final form of political union had yet to be decided, it must accept the Community's political aims. Thus, even though some of the Six, in their internal differences, were raising doubts about monetary union they felt justified in telling a prospective member that it must wholly accept it. The warning about political commitments in the Community was probably also intended as a reminder to Britain.

To reassure the many in Britain who wonder what sort of policies towards the rest of the world might emerge from a Western European political union, the Six point out that their policies towards the East and the West have at all times emphasised the need for conciliation. As long ago as 1959 the Commission laid down a basis for the Community's foreign relations: one of the men who helped to shape the Community, Robert Marjolin, then Vice-President of the Commission, said that it had 'no intention of changing the open, liberal policies we have followed so far and which have given such a sharp stimulus to liberal trade policies and the lowering of tariff barriers throughout the world'.

By 1972 it seemed that growing confidence between Britain, France and West Germany and the other seven members of the enlarged Community would lead to an 'ever closer' political union to help keep the peace in Europe and in the world. While retaining its national spirit Britain may, as President Pompidou has suggested, gradually be convinced that many of its problems, economic, political, strategic and diplomatic, can be solved in a loose confederal framework. Experts differ in their definitions of a confederation. It is most often defined as an association of sovereign states joined for certain common purposes, e.g. defence and external affairs, without having direct power over the associated states.

Sir Alec Douglas-Home is on record as saying that Britain certainly does not want any of this 'federal stuff', that the Community must avoid using such labels and act pragmatically in the field of harmonising foreign policy. He, like his predecessor, Labour's Michael Stewart, favours a cautious step-by-step approach towards political institutions similar to the gradual evolution of most modern British political institutions. Yet at a recent meeting with foreign ministers of the other nine countries of the proposed enlarged Market, Sir Alec played a major role in discussing how national foreign policies could be co-ordinated. West Germany's Walter Scheel appears to have surprised Sir Alec somewhat by putting forward at the same meeting a plan to hasten the creation of political institutions in Brussels. Under this plan each member state of the enlarged Community would be represented, not only by senior economic negotiators, but by top officials from their foreign ministries, who would be permanently established in a Community political committee and would concentrate on preparing proposals for harmonising and ultimately merging foreign policies. This would replace the Davignon Committee which meets in each capital of the Six in turn and has relatively limited powers.

The outcome of these discussions is difficult to forecast. What is certain is that, assuming British entry, foreign and other ministers of the ten countries will, under the Community rules, meet regularly (often once or twice a week) in the Salle Europe in Brussels to determine economic policies and, in the event of a world crisis, to exchange views and prepare joint decisions so that Europe carries weight in world affairs.

The Six have already agreed in principle that a start should be made soon on merging the three Treaties (establishing EEC, ECSC and Euratom) in the manner that their executive bodies have been merged. There would then be an entirely new Treaty in which each country would contribute to the redrafting of the rules needing amendment.

By then, it could well be Britain's turn to take the chair for six months at the Council of Ministers. Britain should also, by then or soon afterwards, be entitled to claim that a British politician should become president of the Commission or be appointed as vice-president in charge of the common agricultural policy or of the economic and monetary union. It is hoped that the European Parliament, enhanced by vigorous debating of British MPs, will acquire more power to ensure a check on Brussels spending and economic and political decision-making.

In saying this, the Six do not rule out that some British representatives may go to Brussels as saboteurs. Britain cannot hope to make the most of its opportunities in the Market if an unconstructive minister is sent during the critical years as full Market rules become applicable in the middle of the five-year transitional period. He should certainly be a good linguist because in difficult bargaining it is frequently helpful to be able to argue in at least two Community languages.

Despite what appears to the observer to be a chaotic process of reaching solutions, the Community is groping forward towards a form of unity which, it now seems, will be an amalgam of the pragmatic and cautious British approach and the more progressive but possibly premature plans of Walter Scheel, often improved by the common sense and idealism of Jean Monnet. It is, as Mr. Heath says, a continuing process.

The Six are already considering a plan for what they call 'institutionalising' their relations with the United States. This means that American and Common Market officials and/or ministers would meet regularly in a Euro-American committee or council to keep each other informed of their problems and attempt to resolve them. There are plans to institutionalise relations between the Market and the Commonwealth, or at least to strengthen them greatly in other ways on the basis of the entry terms.

Britain could, if its representatives in Brussels were sufficiently obtuse, reduce the momentum of the Community and turn it into something similar to EFTA. However, Market officials are hopeful that once Britain is installed it will realise that it is also our Community. Some see the political side of the Community as an extended peace conference that could lead to a peace of the kind that many of the millions who died in the two world wars thought might result from their sacrifice.

Britain is almost certain to begin by assuming a cautious approach to the Community. This approach will become bolder once the Community changes with the assimilation of British attitudes and policies. The result could provide the basis, not only for close economic and political union in Western Europe, but for a step towards a wider framework, some grander design, some form of world order.

STATISTICS OF THE TEN

UNITED KINGDOM

Area: 94,000 sq. mi. **Population:** 55,534,000.

Capital: London (pop. of Greater London 7,703,000). Airport: Heathrow—45 minutes away by car.

Chief cities and ports: Birmingham (1,085,000), Liverpool (677,000), Manchester (594,000), Sheffield (529,000), Leeds (504,000), Hull (293,000), Cardiff (289,000), Newcastle (251,000), Southampton (210,000); Glasgow (928,000), Edinburgh (465,000); Belfast (391,000).

Government: Constitutional monarchy, head of state being the sovereign (hereditary). Executive power vested in cabinet led by prime minister and comprising members of Parliament, which has two Houses: Commons and Lords. Commons contains 630 members and holds ultimate legislative power. Northern Ireland is represented in the Commons, but also has its own Parliament (52 Commons members).

Gross National Product (GNP): £45·6-million. Domestic sources include 45·7 per cent in industry, 3·0 per cent in agriculture (1969 figures).

Employment: Work force totals about 25-million, 8-million of whom are in manufacturing industries. Income per capita: £630 a year. **Cost of living** (retail price index): 155·3 (1962 = 100).

Taxes: Personal tax, standard rate: 38·75 per cent; surtax payable on income over £2,500 on sliding rate. Consumer purchase tax payable on designated list of goods and selective employment tax by service industries (both will be replaced by value-added tax, VAT, in 1973).

Social Welfare: Health contributions: men 16p a week, women 13p. Family allowances: 90p a week for first two children and £1 for every other child. Pension: £6 a week for single person, £9·70 for married couple.

Public Holidays: Good Friday, Easter Monday, Christmas, Boxing Day; New Year's Day in Scotland; Battle of the Boyne (July 12), St. Patrick's Day in Northern Ireland.

Weights and Measures: Imperial system, scheduled for change to metric. One lb. = 0·4536 kilogram; one yard = 0·9144 metre; one gallon = 4·546 litres.

Currency and Exchange Rates: Sterling based on the pound (£); £1 = $2.50 U.S. (approx.).

REPUBLIC OF IRELAND

Area: 27,000 sq. mi. **Population:** 2,921,000.

Capital: Dublin (pop. 569,000). Airport: Dublin—30 minutes away by car.

Chief ports: Cork (122,000), Limerick (56,000), Waterford (30,000).

Government: Head of state is president, elected by direct universal suffrage for seven-year term. Legislature comprises House of Representatives (144 elected members) and Senate (60 members). Executive power vested in cabinet led by prime minister.

Gross National Product (GNP): £1·25-million. Domestic sources include 34·0 per cent in industry, 19·7 per cent in agriculture (1969 figures).

173

Employment: Work force totals just over 1-million, close to 300-thousand of whom are in agriculture. Income per capita: £560 a year. **Cost of living** (consumer price index): 123·6 (1968 = 100).

Taxes: Personal tax, standard rate: 35 per cent; surtax payable on income over £2,500 on sliding rate. Corporate income and corporation tax in process of reducing to 50 per cent. Indirect taxes, consumer five per cent turnover and wholesale ten per cent, replaced by value-added tax (VAT) in March, 1972.

Social Welfare: Health benefits: free medical service for workers earning less than £1,200 and dependants. Social insurance contributions: men £1·68 a week. Family allowance: 50p a month for first child, £1·50 for second, £2·25 for each subsequent child. Pension: £5·50 a week for single person, £9·35 for married couple.

Public Holidays: St. Patrick's Day, Good Friday, Easter Monday, Christmas, Boxing Day.

Weights and Measures: Imperial system (see U.K. fact sheet).

Currency and Exchange Rates: Sterling, at fixed parity with U.K. pound; £1 = $2.50 U.S. (approx.).

FRANCE

Area: 213,000 sq. mi. **Population:** 50,330,000.

Capital: Paris (pop. 2,591,000). Airports: Orly, Le Bourget—45 minutes away by car.

Chief cities and ports: Marseilles (889,000), Lyon (528,000), Toulouse (371,000), Nice (322,000), Bordeaux (267,000), Nantes (259,000), Strasbourg (249,000), Lille (191,000).

Government: Republic, with executive powers vested in president (elected by direct universal suffrage for seven-year term) and council of ministers headed by prime minister. Legislature consists of National Assembly and Senate.

Gross National Product (GNP): £58·4-million. Domestic sources include 48·1 per cent in industry, 6·0 per cent in agriculture (1969 figures).

Employment: Work force totals about 20-million, 5·5-million of whom are in manufacturing, 3-million in agriculture. Income per capita: £743. **Cost of living** (retail price index): 106·5 (1970 = 100).

Taxes: Personal tax, graduated rate: from 0 to 63 per cent. Indirect taxation is applied through value-added tax (VAT), paid on all goods and services at rates varying from between 7 and 35 per cent.

Social Welfare: Health contributions: employee 6·5 per cent of wage, employer 32·2 per cent; benefits based on refund of about 75 per cent of basic doctor's charge. Family allowance: sliding scale, based from birth of first child for couple with one wage-earner and from birth of second child for couple with both wage-earners. Pension: 40 per cent of average wage earned in ten years prior to retirement.

Public Holidays: New Year's Day, Easter Monday, Labour Day, Ascension Day, Whit Monday, Bastille Day (July 14), The Assumption, All Saints', Armistice, Christmas (two days).

Weights and Measures: Metric system.

Currency and Exchange Rates: Basic unit is franc; £1 = 13·80 francs (approx.).

FEDERAL REPUBLIC OF GERMANY (WEST)

Area: 95,000 sq. mi. **Population:** 58,707,000.

Capital: Bonn (pop. 138,000). Nearest airport: Cologne—40 minutes by car.

Chief cities and ports: Hamburg (1,833,000), Munich (1,244,000), Cologne (854,000), Essen (705,000), Dusseldorf (689,000), Frankfurt (622,000), Dortmund (648,000), Stuttgart (614,000), Bremen (604,000), Hanover (527,000); West Berlin (2,163,000).

Government: Federal republic comprises ten states, each represented in legislature by the Bundesrat. Chief legislative organ is Bundestag (elected by direct universal suffrage). Central government led by chancellor, appointed by absolute majority of Bundestag. Each of states has own legislature. West Berlin is separately represented in Bundestag.

Gross National Product (GNP): £64·6-million. Domestic sources include 53·9 per cent in industry, 3·6 per cent in agriculture (1969 figures).

Employment: Work force totals about 22·5-million, of whom 8·6-million are in industry. Income per capita: £1,026. **Cost of living** (retail price index): 123 (1962 = 100).

Taxes: Personal tax, graduated rate: from 23·5 to 53 per cent (56 by 1974). Corporation tax is 56 per cent, with complicated variations.

Social Welfare: Health contributions: employee and employer 8·4 per cent of earnings. Family allowance: from 1974, £6·80 a month for each child up to fifth, after which unstated amount paid. Pension: compulsory scheme for workers earning up to £1,200 a year entitles single person to about £40 a month.

Public Holidays: New Year's Day, Good Friday, Easter Monday, Labour Day, Ascension Day, Whit Monday, Berlin Day (June 17), Pententiary Day, Christmas (two days).

Weights and Measures: Metric system.

Currency and Exchange Rates: Basic unit is Deutsche Mark (DM); set at floating rate in 1971, when £1 = 8·3 DM (approx.).

ITALY

Area: 116,000 sq. mi. **Population:** 53,170,000.

Capital: Rome (pop. 2,602,000). Airport: Leonardo da Vinci (Fiumicino)—one hour away by car.

Chief cities and ports: Milan (1,687,000), Naples (1,257,000), Turin (1,122,000), Genoa (845,000), Palermo (647,000), Bologna (484,000), Florence (455,000), Venice (366,000), Trieste (281,000).

Government: Republic, with president as head of state, elected by two legislative houses, which are Chamber of Deputies (direct universal suffrage) and Senate (regional basis). President nominates council of ministers led by prime minister.

Gross National Product (GNP): £34·25-million. Domestic sources include 38·9 per cent in industry, 11·3 per cent in agriculture (1969 figures).

Employment: Work force totals about 19-million, of whom 8·2-million are in industry and 3·6-million in agriculture. Income per capita: £1,030 a year. **Cost of living** (retail price index): 113 (1970 = 100).

Taxes: Personal tax, based on graduated scale of four categories, from 9 per cent on income of £480 a year to 25 per cent on income of £3,300 a year. Corporation tax is complicated enough to be dealt with by legal experts.

Social Welfare: Health contributions: employees 6·35 per cent.
Family allowance: £3·30 a month for each child and direct dependant. Pension: minimum £15·33 a month for workers insured for at least 15 years.

Public Holidays: New Year's Day, Epiphany, St. Joseph, Easter Monday, Liberation Day (April 25), Labour Day, Ascension Day, Corpus Christi, National Day (June 2), St. Peter and St. Paul, The Assumption, All Saints', National Unity, Immaculate Conception, Christmas, St. Stephen.

Weights and Measures: Metric system.

Currency and Exchange Rates: Basic unit is lira; £1 = 1,500 lira (approx.).

THE NETHERLANDS

Area: 16,000 sq. mi. **Population:** 12,873,000.

Capital: Amsterdam (pop. 846,000). Airport: Schipol—about 40 minutes away by car.

Chief cities and ports: Rotterdam (699,000), The Hague (564,000), Utrecht (276,000).

Government: Constitutional monarchy, head of state being the sovereign (hereditary). Executive power vested in cabinet led by prime minister and comprising members of the legislature, which has two houses: Lower and Upper Chamber. Members of Lower Chamber elected by universal suffrage on proportional representation basis; it has ultimate legislative power.

Gross National Product (GNP): £11·8-million. Domestic sources include 41·6 per cent in industry, 7·0 per cent in agriculture (1969 figures).

Employment: About 40 per cent of work force is in manufacturing and industry and seven per cent in agriculture. Income per capita: £1,070 a year. **Cost of living** (retail price index): 142·1 (1964=100).

Taxes: Income tax, average rate is 40–45 per cent in taxation and social security. Corporation tax is 43–46 per cent of profits. Foreign investors have the same rights as Dutch businessmen.

Social Welfare: Health benefits: free medical, dental, hospital care. Family allowance: £6·67 a month for each child. Pensions: £48·08 a month for a single person and £60·83 for a married couple.

Public Holidays: New Year's Day, Easter Monday, Queen's Birthday (April 30), Ascension Day, Whit Monday, Christmas (two days).

Weights and Measures: Metric system.

Currency and Exchange Rates: Basic unit is guilder; set at floating rate in 1971, when £1 = 8·40 guilders.

BELGIUM

Area: 12,000 sq. mi. **Population:** 9,646,000.

Capital: Brussels (pop. 1,079,000). Nearest airport: Zaventhem—30 minutes away by car.

Chief cities and ports: Antwerp (675,000), Liege (450,000), Ghent (231,000).

Government: Constitutional monarchy, head of state being the sovereign (hereditary). Executive power vested in cabinet led by prime minister and comprising members from legislature, which has two houses: the Senate and Chamber of Deputies. Members of the Chamber elected by universal suffrage on proportional representation basis; nine provinces are represented in Senate.

Gross National Product (GNP): £9·5-million. Domestic sources include 41·6 per cent in industry, 5·3 per cent in agriculture (1969 figures).

Employment: Work force totals about 3·7-million, of whom 1·9-million are in manufacturing and industry. Income per capita: £1,510 a year. **Cost of living** (retail price index): 121·9 (1966=100).

Taxes: Personal tax, average £165 a year; Company tax, average £8,300 a year.

Social Welfare: Social insurance contributions 20 per cent of wages. Medical bills 75–90 per cent refund, free hospitals. Family allowance: £5·50 for first child, £8·50 for second. Pension is linked to cost of living index, aims at 75 per cent of worker's average wage during career.

Public Holidays: New Year's Day, Easter Monday, Labour Day, Ascension Day, Whit Monday, Independence Day (July 21), The Assumption, All Saints', Remembrance Day, Christmas.

Weights and Measures: Metric system.

Currency and Exchange Rates: Basic unit is franc; set at floating rate in 1971, when £1 = 116 francs (approx.).

LUXEMBOURG

Area: 1,000 sq. mi. **Population:** 337,000.

Capital: Luxembourg (pop. 77,000).

Government: Constitutional monarchy, head of state being hereditary prince. Executive powers vested in cabinet led by prime minister and comprising members of legislature, which has two houses: Council of State and Chamber of Deputies.

Gross National Product (GNP): £375,000. Domestic sources include 50·9 per cent in industry and 6·2 per cent in agriculture (1969 figures).

Employment: Work force totals over 150-thousand, of whom 68-thousand are in industry. Income per capita: £1,510 a year. **Cost of living** (retail price index): 117·7 (1966=100).

Social Welfare: Health contributions: employees pay two-thirds of scheme, employers pay one-third. Family allowance: £5·15 for first child, £4·85 for second. Pension is linked to cost of living index, aims at 75 per cent of worker's average wage during career.

Public Holidays: New Year's Day, Easter Monday, May Day, Ascension Day, Whit Monday, National Day (June 23), The Assumption, All Saints', Christmas (two days).

Weights and Measures: Metric system.

Currency and Exchange Rates: Basic unit is Luxembourg franc; set at floating rate in 1971, when £1 = 116 Lf (approx.).

DENMARK

Area: 17,000 sq. mi. **Population:** 4,910,000.

Capital: Copenhagen (pop. 864,000). Airport: Kastrup—15 minutes away by car.

Chief cities and ports: Aarhus (116,000), Odense (107,000), Aalborg (86,000).

Government: Constitutional monarchy, head of state being the sovereign who exercises executive power through cabinet led by prime minister. Unicameral legislature, Folketing, is elected by universal suffrage. Greenland and Faroe Islands represented.

Gross National Product (GNP): £5·83-million. Domestic sources include 40·1 per cent in industry and 8·9 per cent in agriculture (1969 figures).

Employment: Work force totals about 2·35-million, of whom about 600-thousand in manufacturing industry. Income per capita: £688 a year. **Cost of living** (retail price index): 156·8 (1964 = 100).

Taxes: Personal tax, average family pays 25 per cent of income, which, on progressive scale, reaches high of two-thirds of income. Consumer pays 15 per cent value-added tax (VAT), plus extra levy on luxury items. Companies pay 36 per cent tax on annual earnings, with a small deductible allowance.

Social Welfare: Health benefits: free hospital treatment and sick pay. Family allowances: £4·62 a month per child, free education and unemployment pay. Pension: £34·66 a month for single person, £50·83 for a married couple.

Public Holidays: New Year's Day, Maundy Thursday, Good Friday, Easter Monday, Prayer Day, Ascension Day, Whit Monday, Constitution Day (June 5), Christmas (two days).

Weights and Measures: Metric system.

Currency and Exchange Rates: Basic unit is the krone; £1 = 18·09 kroner (approx.).

NORWAY

Area: 125,000 sq. mi. **Population:** 3,851,000.

Capital: Oslo (pop. 484,000). Airport: Fornebu—ten minutes away by car.

Chief cities and ports: Trondheim (121,000), Bergen (117,000).

Government: Constitutional monarchy, head of state being the sovereign. Executive power vested in cabinet headed by prime minister. Legislature, Storting, is elected by universal suffrage. Storting then votes a quarter of its members to the Lagting, remaining three-quarters forming Odelsting.

Gross National Product (GNP): £4·04-million. Domestic sources include 38·6 per cent in industry and 6·5 per cent in agriculture (1969 figures).

Employment: Work force totals about 1·2-million, of whom 378-thousand are in manufacturing industry. Income per capita: £580 a year. **Cost of living** (retail price index): 123·1 (1968 = 100).

Taxes: Personal tax, set in progressive scale, from 15·2 per cent on family income of £580 a year to 47·4 per cent on single person's income of £5,800. Consumer pays 20 per cent value-added tax (VAT), plus extra levy on luxury items. Companies pay 26 per cent tax on net income, plus municipal and developing countries' tax.

Social Welfare: Health benefits: free medical care and sick pay. Family allowances: scaled from £2·42 a month for first child to £11·62 for five children, free education and unemployment pay. Pension: £34·88 a month for single person at age of 70, £52·33 for a married couple.

Public Holidays: New Year's Day, Maundy Thursday, Good Friday, Easter Monday, Labour Day, Ascension Day, Constitution Day (May 17), Whit Monday, Christmas Eve (half day), Christmas.

Weights and Measures: Metric system.

Currency and Exchange Rates: Basic unit is the krone; £1 = 17·06 kroner (approx.).

APPENDIX 1: BALANCE OF PAYMENTS

The effect on Britain's balance of payments as a result of joining the European Community has been the most important individual issue in the negotiations for a great many people in Britain. Estimates of the annual cost to Britain of joining the Community have varied very widely because it is difficult to translate impressions into actual statistical material. The extra cost of imported food in balance of payments terms is estimated at about £5-million in 1973 and £50-million a year by the end of the transitional period. The precise figure depends on undefinable factors, including the extra food which British farmers are persuaded to produce as a result of increased prices.

In addition to the increase in imported food, the balance of payments must also cope with Britain's contributions to the Community budget, largely spent in agricultural price support, the European Social Fund and the administrative costs of running the Community's headquarters in Brussels and Luxembourg. After allowing for net receipts from the Community, the Treasury estimates that Britain's annual contribution will amount to £100-million net in 1973, rising to about £200-million in 1977, when Britain is expected to contribute about £300-million and receive about £100-million.

Under the agreed solution a percentage or 'key' has been set, broadly corresponding to Britain's present share of the total gross national product (GNP) of the ten countries which are forming the enlarged Community. This will represent the proportion of the common budget which Britain should *nominally* be expected to pay in the first year of membership. This key will then increase marginally in each of the four subsequent years, under similar arrangements to those agreed by the Six for themselves.

Britain, however, will pay only a proportion of its *nominal* contribution over these first five years (1973 to 1977). The proportion, as the White Paper explains, will increase in annual steps. The TABLE below shows the effect of these arrangements. Column 2 shows the *nominal* key which has been agreed; Column 3 is the proportion of this nominal key which Britain will in practice pay; Column 5 sets out the possible size of Britain's contributions on the assumption that the budget amounts to £1,400-million in 1973 and rises to

£1,600-million by 1977; Column 6 shows the estimated build-up of Britain's receipts from the budget and the final column shows the estimate of its net payments. (This highly complicated approach to the problem of payments was agreed, negotiators said, because the French insisted on Britain being bound fully by the whole system from the first year of entry.)

(1) Year	(2) United Kingdom key (percentage of Community budget)	(3) Percentage of key to be paid	(4) United Kingdom contribution (percentage of Community budget)	(5) Possible United Kingdom gross contribution (£m.)	(6) Possible United Kingdom receipts (£m.)	(7) Possible United Kingdom net contribution (£m.)
1973	19·19	45·0	8·64	120	20	100
1974	19·38	56·0	10·85	155	40	115
1975	19·77	67·5	13·34	195	55	140
1976	20·16	79·5	16·03	245	75	170
1977	20·56	92·0	18·92	300	100	200

The Community's common budget in 1971 totalled £1,273-million, broken down thus in £ million: European Agricultural Fund 1,096; Community administrative costs 62; repayment to member states to cover costs of collecting levies and duties 56; Euratom research and investment 28; European Social Fund 23; food aid 8.

In 1978 and 1979 Britain's contributions will continue to be controlled by 'correctives' (see Chapter 2, p. 57), and it will not be until 1980 that Britain, for the first time, will be expected to pay its full share of the Community budget.

Answering questions put by Mr. Wilson, Leader of the Opposition, Mr. Rippon said that one figure which had been given was that Britain would have an overall improvement in balance of payments of £1,700-million by the end of the period in which Britain was adjusting to the Community's budget rules. But as well as quoting a plus figure of £1,700-million, a minus figure of £500-million had also been quoted. Mr. Wilson had said this minus figure had been given to journalists but not to the House. Mr. Rippon reaffirmed that no member of the Community would impose an unacceptable burden on Britain.

In 1980 and subsequent years Britain and all other member countries will be expected to pay 90 per cent of the yield of their agricultural levies and their receipts from tariffs on imports from third countries to the Fund, plus a maximum of a one per cent value-added tax. If Britain continues to rely on food and other goods imported from outside the Community, as seems likely, it will pay a proportionately high share of the duties in relation to its share of total output in the Community, which is expected to be just under one-fifth. But to the extent that the Community's activities in agriculture may be reduced and its industrial support operations increased, Britain may expect to receive more of the revenues in future, because of the relatively few inefficient farmers and relatively many industrial regions in need of redevelopment in Britain.

These calculations take no regard of the effects changes in industrial trade may have on the balance of payments. Britain's average external tariff is currently higher than that of the Community, so that some British industries such as machine tools may at first be adversely affected by increased competition A much greater effect is expected as a result of the increase in the tariff-free market opportunities.

Assessments in Whitehall in 1971 estimated that Britain's contributions to the budget and the farm policy would cost Britain probably less than one per cent of the country's current annual output.

The decision accepting the extra balance of payments burden was summed up by Mr. Rippon as a decision to catch up with Europe instead of 'casting adrift'. The alternatives to joining Europe, it was pointed out, have lost much of their appeal. Commonwealth trade as a proportion of Britain's total trade had dwindled. The European Free Trade Association (EFTA) was felt to have been too small to stimulate the British economy. The appeal of a North Atlantic free trade area (NAFTA) decreased as American isolationism increased and because it would mean that Britain was too closely linked, and therefore too dependent, on the Americans. While it was recognized that Britain might fail to meet the challenge of a European environment, the expert view was that it would succeed.

APPENDIX 2: COMMONWEALTH SAFEGUARDS

New Zealand

A derogation from the Community's market organisation rules for dairy products was agreed between Britain and the Six for New Zealand exports of butter and cheese to this country. This derogation was described in an official statement as follows:

1. Quantitative guarantees for imports to Britain of New Zealand dairy products will be fixed for the first five years dating from January 1, 1973. Therefore by 1977 the quantitative guarantee admitted for these products will be 80 per cent of the quantities guaranteed before the transition period for butter, and 20 per cent

for cheese. Expressed as a milk equivalent this represents 71 per cent of the quantities guaranteed before British entry.

2. The price level guaranteed to New Zealand will be the average of that which it enjoyed on the United Kingdom market from 1969 to 1972.

3. From 1978 onwards no further quantitative guarantee will be laid down for cheese.

4. During the third year after British entry the institutions of the Community will review the butter situation in the light of the supply and demand position and trends in the major producing and consuming countries of the world, particularly in the Community and New Zealand. They will take account of New Zealand's progress towards diversification, making it less dependent on butter exports. Progress on effective world agreements on milk products will be considered.

5. In the light of this examination, the Council (on a proposal from the Commission) will decide on suitable measures for ensuring beyond December 31, 1977, the continuation of the derogation system for New Zealand and for determining the details of this system.

Sugar from developing Commonwealth

The Common Market system for sugar combines quotas, support buying and penalties for overproduction. Arrangements are transitional until the end of the 1974 season, and will be renegotiated by the Community with Britain as a member before then. The British entry terms granted by the Six for sugar from the developing countries made these points:

1. Britain's obligations to buy agreed quantities of sugar under Commonwealth Sugar Agreement (CSA) from all participants until the end of 1974 will be fulfilled. After 1974 it is agreed that the arrangements for sugar imports from developing Commonwealth sugar-producing countries should be in the framework of an agreement allowing them to become associate members of the Market or to have special trade links with it. India's arrangements would be negotiated separately.

2. The enlarged Common Market would have 'as its firm purpose' the safeguarding of the interests of the developing countries concerned whose economies depended to a considerable extent on the export of primary products and in particular sugar. The countries concerned: Antigua, Barbados, Fiji, Guyana, India, Jamaica, Kenya, Mauritius, Swaziland, Trinidad and Tobago, Uganda, St. Kitts-Nevis-Anguilla and British Honduras.

APPENDIX 3: ECONOMIC AND MONETARY UNION

With great difficulty the Six agreed in February 1971 on a *three-stage outline plan aimed at full economic and monetary union by the end of 1980*.

Stage 1 (1971–3) of the economic and monetary union plan would necessitate:

> Narrowing of margins between their currency exchange rates.
>
> Setting up a medium-term support fund of 2,000-million dollars to meet member states' balance of payments difficulties.
>
> Co-ordination of short and medium-term economic and budgetary policies.
>
> Regular meetings of Common Market finance ministers and heads of their central banks.
>
> Moving towards a joint position on international monetary issues.
>
> Further moves to harmonise taxation in Market countries.
>
> Discussion of proposals for a European Monetary Co-operation Fund.
>
> Moves to hasten the development of the poorer regions of the Common Market.

As part of a compromise aimed at healing a breach between West Germany and France it was decided that at the end of 1973, as Stage 1 was due to end, the Six would decide on the ultimate nature of the economic and monetary union and set out developments for Stage 2 (1974–6). The Six said they hoped to decide whether to transfer national control of economic policies to Community institutions, including the European Parliament. Their three-stage plan was to a large extent based on reports prepared by M. Pierre Werner, Luxembourg Prime Minister, and M. Raymond Barre, member of the Commission.

APPENDIX 4: EUROPEAN COMMUNITIES BILL

The European Communities Bill, published on January 26, 1972, brings United Kingdom regulations into line with those of the three Communities Britain is joining: the Common Market, Coal and Steel Community and Euratom (atomic energy).

Clause 1, after listing these Communities, refers to the Treaties to which Britain shall accede and covers any future treaties.

Clause 2, regarded as the heart of the Bill, covers the implementation of Britain's obligations and rights and provides for changes in British law to meet them.

Paragraph 1 says: 'All such rights, powers, liabilities, obligations, and restrictions from time to time created or arising by or under the Treaties, and all such remedies and procedures from time to time provided for, by or under the Treaties, as in accordance with the Treaties are without further enactment to be given legal effect . . .'

Paragraph 2 provides that powers exercised in Community institutions cannot impose taxes, make retrospective provisions to provide further delegation of powers, or create new criminal offences. A schedule to the Bill lays down that any such order or regulation can be annulled by a vote in either the Commons or the Lords.

Paragraph 3 covers financial provisions for payments and receipts.

Clause 3 provides that any legal determination of the Treaties' meaning will be governed by principles laid down by the European Court. In the fields covered by the Treaties, British courts should take note of the Treaties, the Official Journal of the Communities and judgments of the European Court.

Part 2 of the Bill sets out amendments of British law needed to meet Community requirements.

Clause 5 defines Britain's commitments to the customs union on which the Common Market is based: included is the provision that revenue collected by British customs will no longer belong to the Crown as member states pay it into the Community's central fund. Under a schedule to the Bill, importers will have one month's credit before paying in customs dues.

Clause 6 establishes an intervention board, appointed by the minister of agriculture, for agricultural produce. The board will collect agricultural levies as provided for in the Common Market policies and run the systems linked with maintaining farm prices in Britain at Market levels.

The remaining Clauses, 7–12, cover acceptance of Market rules in such sectors as sugar, company law, the composition and labelling of food, and the grading of horticultural products.

INDEX

Italics used to denote main discussion of topic

Deutsche Mark, revaluation of 85, 103

dividends, taxation on 111

dollar, devaluation of the (1971) *104*

Douglas-Home, Sir Alec 19, 154, 168, 170

duties: common budget 91; CET 8, 9, 11; countervailing 89; EFTA 26; excise 111; industrial tariffs 63–4; national tariff 68; variable import levy 90

duty-free allowances *166*

economic and monetary union 8, *103–5, 183*; Council of Ministers 10

Economic and Social Committee 34; CAP 97, unions 83

economic policies, integration of *103–5*

ECSC *see* European Coal and Steel Community

Education, Ministry of *158*

EEC *see* European Economic Community

Environment, Ministry for 158

EFTA *see* European Free Trade Association

eggs: price increases 92; sluice-gate prices 89

electrical plant *65*

energy: Community of Ten production (graph) 119; ECSC *68–70*; Euratom *70–1*; special policy needs *71–3*

engineering, general *65–6*

entry terms: CET 9; Rome Treaty *32–59*; legislation for implementation 13

equal pay for women 162

Euratom *see* European Atomic Energy Community

Euratom Treaty *30*

Europe, Action Committee for the United States of 25

European Agricultural Guidance

and Guarantee Fund (FEOGA): CAP 91; regional development 105

European Atomic Energy Community (Euratom) 10, 25–6, *70–1*, 171

European Coal and Steel Community (ECSC) 10, 23–5, *68–70*, 72, 171; powers 68–70; regional development 105

European Confederation of Free Trade Unions 83

European Court of Justice 7, 14, 22; Britain 31, 160; Commission 11; Rome Treaty *34*

European Economic Community (EEC) 7–8, 10, *33–59*, 171; checks and balances 16; commercial policy 111–13; powers 8, 11; regional policy *73–4*, 104–5

European Free Trade Association (EFTA) 26–7, 60, 113

European Human Rights Court 118

European Investment Bank 34, 51–2, 74; regional development 105

European Parliament 7, 11, *14*, 22; British contribution 168, 171; CAP 97; Commission dismissal 14, 158; economic policy 104; Youth Office 166; federalists 20; legislative powers 15; strengthening of 158

European Social Fund: regional development 34, 74, 105

everyday consequences of British entry *160–6*

fall-back price *see* reserve price

family allowances *81*

farming, British prospects 93–100

farming, Irish prospects 127

fats: price increases 92

federalists 19, *20–5*, 156; armed forces 20, 25; Euratom 25; defence 25, 155–6; European Parliament 20, 22; government 156; reserve bank 20